The Principles of Sahaj Marg

Volume XII

by

Shri P. Rajagopalachari

(President, Shri Ram Chandra Mission)

Shri Ram Chandra Mission

Shahjahanpur, (U.P.) 242 001

India

First Edition: April, 1999
Copies: 7000

ISBN 81 86553 66 5 (Vol. XI)
ISBN 81 85177 01 5 (Set)

Price Rs. 100.00

Publishers:
SHRI RAM CHANDRA MISSION
Shahjahanpur, (U.P.) 242 001
INDIA

Printed at:
Nagaraj and Company Private Limited
153-A, Lattice Bridge Road,
Thiruvanmiyur,
Chennai 600 041

Publishers' Note

We are here, once again, with the next collection of our Revered and Beloved Master, Pujyashri Parthasarathi Rajagopalachari's speeches and talks given in India during his extensive travel to all parts of the country.

This collection covers talks in the first half of the calendar-year 1990, beginning with the New Year speech at Madras. It contains the messages of both the Basant Utsav held at Bombay as well as the Babuji Birthday Celebrations held at Jaipur in April 1990. Also included is the talk given to students followed by a question–and answer session which was broadcast over the television on the national network.

We are sure our eager readers will enjoy this collection immensely.

Publications Department
Shri Ram Chandra Mission

Contents

The River of Life

Dear Brothers and Sisters,

We have heard a lot of talk. Of course, we listen to the things with some sense of purpose. The talk should not only be purposeful, meaningful, and useful, but it should also be digestible, like food. I was wondering, when one of the speakers was speaking about this thing, which we are all familiar with, that whether we eat good food or bad food, when there is too much food there is diarrhoea. We normally think only bad food gives us a bad stomach. But good food also gives a bad stomach, if we eat too much. Anybody will know that if we eat a whole bar of Toblerone chocolate, we are sick—a very expensive sickness! It is the same thing if we eat two *idlis* extra. So, it is not the quality of food that determines anything; it is how much of it we eat. Because if we eat less, even of a bad thing, it will not do so much harm; it could do some good. That is the principle of homeopathy, where they have, they call them poisons, which have been reduced to such a minimum dose that they start working as curing agent, a curative agent.

So, I don't think nature really recognises any difference between good and bad, between darkness and light. What I am trying to suggest is that, in Nature, there is no duality. We talk of snakes with poison but, for instance, for the snake there is no

---

Talk at Chennai on 1 January, 1990

1

poison. It is in it. There are poisonous fruits, mushrooms, which are deadly poisonous. But the mushroom itself does not die. So, why should we die if we take a little poison? Because there is no compatibility. "What is sauce for the goose is sauce for the gander," says the old English proverb. But it is crazy, like most of the English proverbs! When you really go deep into the meaning they are all stupid. What is sauce for the goose need **not** be sauce for the gander. "One man's food is another man's poison," says another proverb. They are two opposite proverbs!

So let us try to understand that in Nature, there is no poison, there is no salt, no sweet, no light, no darkness. These are all what we feel, and the way in which we interpret our environment and our existence. It must also follow that there is no happiness and sorrow. That too is a subjective interpretation by our own mind of a situation, of an event. And because we are subjectively concerned with our own selves, we suffer or enjoy, both of which are again non-sensical. There can be no suffering; there can be no enjoyment.

The whole purpose of spirituality is to evolve from a merely human existence where all this duality is sort of drummed from both the sides: good-bad, light-darkness, heat-cold—we have been thumped from both sides. As one of our sayings in Tamil says, it is like a percussion instrument being beaten with both hands, on both sides, all the time; it is taking a beating all the time. But, as my Master used to say, in taking a beating it produces a lovely rhythm. And all that we do is to produce a lot of noise, which upsets everybody else. So, if you have to be beaten, make sure that the noise you make is at least pleasant for other people to hear so that they can enjoy even your sorrow, even your bewailing, even your sickness. Why should we weep? Because we are angry? Because we are afraid or we are tired? Because we are sick? My Master always said that in nature no animal weeps. A frog is confronted by a snake and it is just waiting till is killed. It is petrified, we say. That is how we interpret; we don't know. We have never been a frog before a snake. So, before we use all these examples—some of these cultivated people in the West, they are always worried about the health of their dogs and cats: "Poor thing, my cat is suffering so much." How do you know? If you had been a saint, you would have gone into the body of the cat and experienced what it feels and would have known by actual personal experience!

What the West calls evolution, where the life-forms begin in some ordinary unicellular organism in the oceans and comes up to the present level of human beings through all those various forms, is perhaps, the need to experience life at various levels, and is not necessarily evolution. I am beginning to question the concept of evolution itself. When a child goes through the various grades in school, he is only being educated. He is not evolving. He is **experiencing** education at its various levels from what you call the lowest to what you call the highest, not **necessarily** the lowest and the highest. When you climb up a staircase, is there a lower step and a higher step? Each step, if you take individually, doesn't look any different from the rest. So what is the lower and what is the higher step? They are all the same steps, the same marble, or the same piece of stone, or same piece of gold, if you are having a golden staircase. Yet we make the foolish mistake of thinking that this is the lower, and this is the first step, and that is the second step. The step can say, "Damn fool! What do you mean by lower and higher step? What is the difference between this step and that step? Can you show me the difference?" So it is only a difference of position for us, for a human being. One step leads to the other. There is no such thing as a lower step and a higher step. It leads you where you wish to go. If you are going down, it is still the right step. When a man comes down from top floor to the ground floor, he needs the lower steps. Can you only keep going up and not coming down? Then it will be like one of those delightful woodcuts by Escher, where you go round and round and you are always going up. Apparently such a staircase has never been built. So to give up these ideas of good and bad, wise and foolish, high and low, I think will take a lot of time, because through the evolutionary processes we have learnt to think of life-forms themselves as high and low.

I can't imagine why an amoeba, for instance, should be low life-form, and we, a higher life-form. If you ask an amoeba, it will laugh at us! The amoeba will say, "Foolish fellow, you are spending fourteen hours a day earning money to feed yourself. I don't have to do anything! Another fourteen hours you are spending foolishly searching for a mate; I just divide. You are multiplying, I am just dividing. Who is wiser? You have to eat and digest, have these problems of stomach and the liver this and that. I just go round my food and it is finished!" Now if I were an amoeba, I could teach you a lot of things and sort of prick the bubble of your ego in so many places, you see! And I could surely make every one of you wish, or at least most of you wish that, "How nice it would be to be an amoeba?" First of all, men would think, "Thank Heaven we don't need women any more," and the women would think, "Thank Heaven we don't need men any more." There would be a huge sigh of relief!

So this is all crazy, subjective evaluation of the truth. The only truth perhaps finally we will find out is: there is no truth. Because truth is also relative. You are told to tell certain things when you are young; you are told to change when you are old; you are told to say yet other things when you are older. When you come to my age, perhaps then you will say, "Well, this is the truth." When I am going to be eighty? For Heaven's sake, I don't know what will be the truth then!

One thing I have learnt from Lord Krishna's life is that there is no "standard" life. As Kannan was just trying to indicate—he didn't go ahead with full courage. That Lord of ours was a crook! There was nothing he did not do which could not be called straightforward and honest. Everything he did had a purpose. But if the purpose is right, perhaps the means have to be the way they have to be. When human beings build canals, they build them straight. But when nature goes round and round, taking curves and turns, and goes round rocks, up and down, you don't call the river a crooked river! It finds its way. So why should a man, who finds his course through life like that, be called crooked? In fact, there is no straight line in nature. A straight line is a human creation. Everything in nature is a curved trajectory. Even a bullet doesn't go in a straight line. It is a stupid thing to say, "As straight as an arrow's flight." When you take a short span, it seems to be straight. Like any circle big enough, if you take a section of it, it appears to be a straight line, but it is, really speaking, a curvature.

So we go by so many of these, what I can only call orthodox stupidities. Each society has them, each religion has them, each culture has them, and each philosophy has them in profundity, you see. "In profound absurdity," is a definition of philosophy.

In this situation, if I have to evolve and not to be pulled this way or that...I find in society two sets of people. People who are afraid of doing wrong and are always are praying like hell to some God, whom they have never seen, in whom they have no faith, whom they don't trust: "Please save me from sin." The other half merrily doing sin and praying to that same God: "Forgive me for my sins." Now, of the two, perhaps the sinner is better. As Babuji has written somewhere: "Don't you believe in God's mercy that you are afraid to sin?" A very profound statement. It is in the Urdu language. It is not Babuji's original. It is of one of the poets in the Urdu tradition, who is asking a man whose mind wants to sin, but he is not sinning, "Why are you so, torturing yourself

always with the idea of sin and trying to avoid it?"
And it makes sense, because the sins of the mind
are more than that of the body. After all, everything
originates in the mind. And if you can regulate the
mind, which is the purpose of raja yoga, there is no
need for any God after that.

Why Sahaj Marg can say, without any sense of
despotism of the Master or unfaithfulness to the
divine Creator, that we don't need God, that He has
no mind? It is not some futile statement of an
atheist. It is a profound statement, arising out of an
individual experience of an absolute believer in a
Creator, who says, "Only he who is still conscious of
sin and virtue needs a God, either to save him or to
protect him, to bless him or to reward him." "I am
beyond both," says my Master, "Which God should I
be afraid of? Which God should I go after as if I am
begging him for gifts?" "God! I have been doing well.
Give me ten rupees"—like a taxi driver, like the
porter at the railway station. We want neither to beg
nor to give as if we are giving to beggars.

In Sahaj Marg there is only one truth: That we
are a part of that divine essence. No different from
the divine totality, except in this fact, that, it is like
a cup of water taken out of the ocean which,
because it is contained in the cup, feels isolated,
small, uncontented. "I am not free," the water in the
cup says. The ocean laughs and says, "Come back
into me. Then you will be the ocean!"

It is very unfortunate that our scientific
education, as much as our theological or other
education, makes stupid fools of us all. Evolution is
a disgrace to this world and we give Nobel prizes to

7

these people! So we must avoid science as much as we should avoid superstitions. As my great mentor, Dr. Varadachari used to say, "Science is also a superstition." This is scientific superstition, that is unscientific superstition. This is irrational superstition, that is rational superstition. That molecules and atoms exist is a superstition; they are assumptions. The great scientists, if you go through their lives and their biographies and their literature, don't say atoms or molecules and sub-molecules or particles exist. They say, assuming that they exist, so many things can be explained. Nobody has ever seen these things. They are just images or streaks left behind somewhere, valuable as clues. It is like the footprints on the beach in the life of that fellow isolated in an island—Robinson Crusoe. He was blissfully alone. After many years, one day he walked around the beach and he found the footsteps of another, and it terrified him. His peace was lost. His serenity was shattered. His isolation was broken. He put his foot into it and measured—it was not his foot! Immediately he started building a barricade, although it was a human foot!

So company makes us sick; lack of company makes us sick. Sometimes you want to be alone; sometimes you want to be with others. So, what is the value of company in itself? It depends upon what I am at that moment. There is no such thing as, "Company is always nice. Come along, let us have a jolly time." A jolly time depends upon you; a sorrowful time depends on you. The same man, the same circumstances can be miserable one day and absolutely ecstatic another day. So where lies happiness and joy, misery, all these things? It is here. So, to say that man is an animal is wrong. He can be having such tendencies at one moment. And to say he is divine is also stupid, because at some time he has these impulses of goodness, generosity, kindness, charity and mercy. Those ideas seem to be and must be to give up all dualities and become in ourselves that which we have to become. Not to become like God, or be God, or merge with God. I think even merger is with the self. Instead of evolution, it is an **involutionary** process. I would dare to suggest today, that what Sahaj Marg really teaches is how to become an involutionary being. Go into yourself! You know, some of these things which children blow into—a coiled up tube. When you blow into it, it opens out; when you let out air, it comes back. We have been evolving from an amoeba, or before the amoeba, to these gigantic, stupendous, attractive human beings, and where is He? What are our miseries? How much misery have we created for ourselves and for others? How much danger? How much solitude in the midst of a crowd, how much loneliness, how much penury in the centre of plenty? I mean, such a wide dualism never existed before.

Today, on one side they are creating plenty, on the other side there is more abject poverty. On one side, the brilliance of the mind, on the other the absolutely decadent, perverted intelligence, which can create vast machines for destruction of self and otherwise. We are widening this rift of dualism. So today, we find examples of either extremes. The medium line does not exist. Therefore, when elite people, really enlightened elite, the spiritually enlightened elite, speak to us, they speak of the need to bring the edges closer and closer. Don't widen these gaps, narrow them. Throw away this and throw away that, too. It must be true. If there is a well-balanced plank on a fulcrum, and if you cut one metre here, you have to cut one metre there, too; otherwise it cannot remain balanced. I have suggested this once earlier. Progressively we have to cut both ends until we come to the fulcrum, and there is nothing on it any more. But we are going in the technological way, in the modern educational way, widening this pole. The two extremes are going further and further away from us. Therefore you find frantic searches for either extremes. If in the old days you could get drunk on just the juice of the toddy plant, which you find in the palms, today you need very strong alcohol. If in the old days a little ginger could cure your stomach ache, today you need antibiotics. Why? Because we have taken this diversionary path, diverging all the time.

I am something; I pretend to be something else. Because inside I am something and outside something else. The inner me is becoming more and more distant from the outer me. Therefore schizophrenia, for instance. How can it be otherwise? So forget all this business. That is God's business. If He exists, let Him exist, let Him be happy. What is our business? Just to go before God in a temple or some religious place and to weep and wail and beat our breast and pretend we are sinners? Nobody really pretends they are sinners. Even when they confess in church they are doing it

Master in Manapakkam Ashram

Master with abhyasis in Chennai

only out of mere formality. If it is a real confession from the heart, they would never repeat the same mistake again. It is a formality and that damn fool, sitting inside in his cassock, is blessing you with the cross. Another formality! "In the name of the Father and the Son and the Holy Ghost, I absolve you from your sins." For Heaven's sake, what power does he have to absolve you of your sins? Therefore, we come out as sinful as we went in, no better than we went in, still in doubt whether my sins are being removed or not, and then we say, "To hell with it. If it is still there, let me do some more!"

See, there is faithlessness in every walk of life. It is another way of saying there is another hypocrisy. The priest is hypocritical, then the confessor, the judge is hypocritical, right up to the top—involving itself in fields it should not. Politics should never be the consideration of the church. And politics, per-contra, should never have to do anything with religion. When these two meet, they make strange and ill bed companions.

Therefore, in Sahaj Marg we have this absolute stipulation that we don't involve ourselves in political activities at all, at any level. The only thing we have in political life is once in four or five years we cast our vote, which is our democratic function. I won't say it is right, I won't say it is duty, I won't say it is a privilege. It is to keep society running. As in old days, Hindu fathers had to have one child, not out of sense of duty or this or that but the duty to the race to keep it running. The stream must flow. Please remember that you have several duties and the duty to yourself is the paramount duty. Because as long as you consist of what you are and remain what you are, you are not going to help humanity one whit. Whether you are a most erudite professor of this world does not matter. You may teach facts; you don't give them education. You may teach principles; you don't make them ethical. You may tell moral examples; you don't make them moral. A teacher who only teaches facts, but cannot change the students who come before him is not worth the salt that he eats. And we as students, when we go before them, if we don't change, there is something seriously wrong. Because it is my contention that you can change even with the worst, stupid teacher that you can have, so long as you go with the intention of changing yourself. I mean, when you go for a bath, a shower, the water does not know what it has to do. It is an insensible object. It does not say, "Aha! He has come, let me clean him thoroughly." It just flows, and we utilise it. Why cannot you utilise fools? Why cannot we use disaster? Why cannot we use sickness? We can, absolutely.

This is one of the great teachings of my Master. It is embedded in our maxims: "Take miseries as divine blessings." If you eat one bar of Toblerone and you fall sick, next time you should not do it. It is a lesson that Toblerone taught you, and you should say "Tobler, thank you." Whoever the Tobler may be, he has taught me something: how not to eat attractive things too much. But we don't learn the lesson. Next time, when you eat a whole bar all over again, somebody will say, "Last time you had..." "Oh! That was because of something else. It was the water, I think, in Chari's house." It is never the Toblerone, because you like it too much. A man becomes drunk. If you ask him, "What happened?" He will say, "Oh people think it is because of the beer. You know, it is the best German beer. How can it be the beer? It must have been something I had just before that, you know. These two did not combine well." This attitude of justifying ourselves to ourselves, justifying mistakes, justifying stupidity, justifying ignorance, justifying evil knowing it is evil, is what is keeping us not only where we are, but probably pushing us more and more down.

So the greater philosophy of Sahaj Marg is this: Don't fool yourself. As my Master used to say, there is no harm in telling lies to others. Don't tell lies to yourself.

I have some abhyasis in the rest of the world, who are trying to tell me lies, telling themselves lies all the time. I have abhyasis here too, who are telling the same thing, but this is more threatening to me, because it comes from people who are supposed to be respectable, educated, moneyed people, successful people. You know, it is always rather intriguing, rather nauseating, when you find these things in so-called respectable people. When a robber robs, we are not so surprised. After all, he is a robber. But if the Prime Minister of the country is amassing gold in a Swiss bank, we are shocked, because he is supposed to protect us, our resources, and he himself is swindling. When this hiatus between preaching and practising becomes too much, it is always a danger. Therefore beware of

13

these preachers who tell you something and do something else; offer you something and give you something else. Beware! But even more to be beware of is your own divergence, from what you are to what you pretend to be. Damn the teacher! After all, it is his problem, it is his responsibility. He will have his fate. But what about us?

So, the sooner we come to bridge this gap between what I am and what I ought to be and what I pretend to be, and bring these all into one, that is the real integration of the self. Forget all these psychological theories of bringing this and this together, that and that together, removing this and substituting that. That is all mechanical. It is like Lego bricks with which we build houses. They don't exist.

Finally, I should offer you an image I read about recently, of a river. I am always fascinated by the rivers. One sage has said that life is like a river. Good on one side, bad on the other. As banks between which the water flows are there to guide us, and the water should not flow over either bank but should be contained, so also should we be contained by this idea of good and bad as two limiting extremes, within which we should move. If you are able to do that without being affected by the concept of good and bad, without relating it to yourself, because the water that is rubbing against this bank which you call good, or the water which flows past that bank which you call bad, is not getting contaminated by either the good or the bad, but it is using both the banks to contain it so that the water is not wasted. The water does not spill over it. It is not a danger to other people. Yet between them it manages to flow through and reach the destination which is the sea.

This should be our life. Let us hope we all get moulded in that way and throw away guilt, throw away also the opposites, of self pride: "No, I have done nothing wrong." Such a person doesn't exist. Neither the highest saints, nor the lower saints, nor the lowest criminals, nor the lowest sinners. All are equal.

Remember, I have said several times that life is a school. If I have failed in one school, it is my failure. The teacher doesn't fail me. I have failed. If I am not allowed to go to the next class, it is because, if I cannot handle this class, how will I handle the next class? Therefore, I am detained here until I master this class and I must prove, I must be able to accept more responsibility of a higher standard of education of the next class. Promotion is no reward. Being retained in the same class is no punishment. It is a second chance for us to equip ourselves more fully to go up in the ladder. A man who cannot operate at the lower level in a bank cannot possibly operate at a higher level in the bank. It is not a punishment, it is not a promotion. As we qualify ourselves, by internal change, by going nearer and nearer, this concept that the divinity exists within us, so our life will proceed in one way. You may call it progress, you may call it evolution, you may call it growth—call it what you will, but it is what it is.

Thank you.

Spiritual Expansion

There were some of our more pessimistic brothers who said that there would not be many people present today, because they would be making *pongal* and eating it at home. Actually, I was happy in the morning because this part of the hall at least was full. But many people seem to have gone away since then.

I had one thought about this hall: it is a fairly big hall and can seat five hundred people. Suppose our land was extending only, say, one metre on all sides of this hall, and we had to build a wall or a compound, we would feel so hemmed in. The hall would be the same but our field would be totally different, because a limit has been set. It is funny, isn't it, that you have the same hall, but just because your land is only one metre on each side, you feel it is small. When there is no limit, you feel it is big.

So the big-ness or the smallness is not in what we have, but in the limits that are imposed by other circumstances. I hope you appreciate this point. It is fairly simple; nothing to think about. It is not philosophy in any case; just a bit of mundane experience. And if there were no walls at all, we would feel absolutely free. You have only to look at the nomads, the people who take out their animals and live in the upper reaches of the hills. As poets would put it, they live under the sky, beneath the stars. And their tribe is supposed to be wonderful precisely because, not that there is anything wonderful in the sky or the stars—they are there, they will always be there. It is because of that sense of freedom that we get when there are no limits. Spirituality says, widen your limiting boundaries as much as you can, until you can destroy them.

Now, the second thought I have to offer you is about the heart. Why the Master's heart? One, of course, because His heart has no limits; it has no boundaries; in fact, it is not a heart at all. It is an unbounded space, which if you wish to think of it that way, has the essence of the heart in it. It is like a perfume. If you open the bottle, you can smell it everywhere; if you keep it closed, there is no perfume. You have just to walk through the streets of Paris: millions of bottles of the most expensive perfumes, but there is no smell anywhere, because they keep everything tightly closed, packed up in small and big cartons, cellophane round it, then another piece of paper and a ribbon on top. It is imprisoned perfume! Whereas you go through the Indian bazaar, you smell everything everywhere: you smell the spices, you smell the cow-dung, you smell the perfume, and you smell the flowers, precisely because there is no limit. The perfume is everywhere.

Now, interestingly enough, two days back, we were walking in our morning walk and somebody said that all smells were not the same—cow-dung and Chanel No. 5 cannot be the same. I said, "Yes, the only difference is, cow-dung is free and

Chanel No. 5 is two hundred and fifty francs for five millilitres." Almost rupees five hundred! It is crazy! It is almost ten rupees to a drop! This lady said, "What is the difference?" I said, "No difference."

When you have a spectrum of colours: violet, indigo, blue, green, yellow, orange, and red, you don't say, "This is a dirty colour and that is a beautiful colour." They are all colours of one spectrum. Similarly we have a spectrum of smells that we can smell. There are smells which we cannot smell, which go beyond the perfume and below the cow-dung also. So nature has filters which only make us see through a slit. Like what we see is colour; what we smell is smell; what we touch are sensations. Now, if there is no good colour and bad colour, why should there be a good smell and a bad smell? It is because we have used our wonderful human intelligence and our sense of aesthetics to say, "This is good and that is bad." Therefore the saint says, "There is no good smell, there is no bad smell; there is no good colour, there is no bad colour." Similarly, you have a spectrum of human beings: something on the violet side of the spectrum, something on the infrared side of the spectrum. They are all human beings. Like colour changes through the spectrum, like smell changes through the spectrum, like sensations change through the spectrum—something is prickly, something is soft— human beings also constitute the spectrum and it is stupid to say that some are good, some are bad.

This is the important teaching of Sahaj Marg. I prefer to limit it to Sahaj Marg very deliberately because even in the so-called *sanatana* dharmic tradition, there is always this question of raising the sinner, cleaning the dirty, and all sorts of nonsense. Even they create some sort of an artificial distinction between good and bad, between virtue and vice, and things like that. It is my great pleasure that in Sahaj Marg we don't have these concepts. We have only the concept of grossness and no grossness. There is no such thing as bad grossness and good grossness. I have always been telling the Western people that if two people have diarrhoea, one getting it out of eating something bad and another getting it out of eating the most expensive chocolate on earth, diarrhoea is still diarrhoea. The rich man cannot pride himself in saying, "Mine is Toblerone diarrhoea, yours is some stupid Indian diarrhoea." Only fools will talk like that!

So, we don't have this question, or distinction of saints and sinners, the virtuous and vicious, the good and the bad, the wise and the unwise. My Master taught that everything is samskara. And what samskara we have is reflected in our actions, in our thoughts. Therefore the most important thing is to recognise, as Rene Tosti said, the unity of life, because philosophy says if there were no good, you would not know what is bad. Per contra, if you know there was nothing which is called bad, you would not know what is good either. And since God, by definition, is only one—there cannot be a second *Ekam Advitiyam*—nothing else exists except God. Therefore, they have this maya philosophy, *Mayavada* as they call it, that everything else is illusory. Not illusion, but an illusory existence.

We are here for the moment, for the time being, like fireflies in the night. If He is only one, how can you say He is good or He is bad? How can you call Him cruel? How can you also call Him kind? To say He is kind is as stupid to say He is cruel; to call Him beautiful is as stupid as to call Him ugly. He cannot be anything. This truth, Sahaj Marg very forcibly emphasises that God is nothingness. Of nothingness, you cannot say it is complete nothingness or incomplete nothingness, or nothing nothingness. You cannot define it; you cannot quantify it; you cannot qualify it.

Sahaj Marg does not preach about unity of human beings or unification of human beings; it does not preach social unity. It does not preach a religion of opportunities for the same: all for the same opportunity; the same opportunity for all. There is really no socialism also involved in Sahaj Marg. I say this because the other day we had an argument with one of our Western brothers, who unfortunately is missing today, who claimed that India is socialist. Yes, but our socialism is something else. It is not a political socialism. It is the socialism of the Divine, if I can say that, where in the vision of the great men of India, they saw no distinction. Not only between human beings, but not also between animals, not between insects, not between this whole gamut of existence. For them, an insect, a cow, an elephant, or a human being, all were the same.

Life is life. That the form is different does not mean life is different. Some chocolates are round, some are square, some are triangular, and some are pyramidal. Yet they are all chocolates. Of course, some people are like children. They want the gold covered, coin-type chocolates like they sell in Switzerland! It looks like a big golden coin. But inside it is the same chocolate!

So if you could spiritually dissect any form of life—I am now not talking about the dissection that we do in our laboratory, just about the carapace—exposing the muscular system, cutting it open; exposing the nervous system, cutting it open; exposing the visceral system...—not that. If you could spiritually dissect, you would find the same inner existence, the essence of existence. You call it the soul, you call it the *atman,* it is the same in all forms. This is the socialism that India presents. The oneness—that everything is found in the unity of everything—the essential oneness! When we are taught this lesson and we are able to accept it with our hearts, we begin to love life. Not to respect life—I beg to differ in this statement that we have to have respect for life, because respect can mean a different thing. We have a love of life. Not the love of your own life, which everybody has, but the love of Life—no qualification.

Therefore you have this great and most noble principle of *ahimsa* [non-violence] in our culture here: Not causing harm or pain to any living form. It is not that we pretend to be Gods or saints in this country. It is because of yet another belief that what you do will inevitably have its reflection in you.

If you love life, life will love you, which means that for such a person there is immortality, because his life will not want to leave him or her. Now, when

21

we look at our lives as endued in a body, this dualism of life and the body which it occupies, it is quite possible my life hates my body. If I myself hate my body: I think it is ugly, I think it is stupid, I think it is corrupt, how much more should my life hate that body? And then should it not be justified in wanting to leave this dirty body behind and go off into its own freedom? Is it therefore not surprising that such people die young—they don't need disease!

So, it is not enough that we love life. Life must love us to such an extent that the life that is within me, should say, "I shall not leave this fellow. I love him so much." But you say, "Yes, this is corrupt," and He says "Don't worry, leave that to me. You do your job. You get better and better and you become more and more fit for me to exist in you."

We have to make ourselves fit enough for the Self within us to continue to exist within us. For such a person, there is no death. Immortality is all nonsense, if you think of some empyrean or some sort of a Greek Heaven full of damsels and wine! That is an escapist idea of Heaven; that is an escapist idea of immortality. The true immortality means no more mortal existence. Because, however good your house, you like to go out of it. Even kings in a palace are often fed up and want to go and live in a jungle, in a cottage like this.

So that is the whole essence of Sahaj Marg: Limits must go. First, the limits must be expanded; second, the limits must be made beautiful, acceptable, incorruptible. Therefore people make strong walls around properties; they should not be made of mud which water will dissolve. This is a question of a continuing effort. People imagine that in Sahaj Marg once they get the first three sittings, their job is over!

Now, somebody was talking about a new beginning: that Babuji had an ashram there, somebody is building an ashram here, yet somebody will begin another ashram somewhere else. So, if you follow this thought in the right sense, it only means that we begin things, we never end things. I believe that only God or Nature has the right to begin and to end. We have a right only to begin; what the end will be, is in His hands. Therefore we say, "Begin it," and don't think of the result because the result is an end. A result is something you get at the end of a process, at the end of a series of efforts or .one single effort, at the end of a cycle of occupation or intense work. But when we have no right to end, but only to begin, and the end is not there, the result cannot be there.

How great must be the wisdom of that Lord of the Gita, Lord Krishna, who said, "Don't think of the result. That is mine." It is foolish to say, "I want my result," because you are cutting something artificially which has no end. The result will be only at the real end. And what is the real end? When my life's journey is finished, when I am merged back into the Centre from which I came, from the source from which I came. That result is inevitably the same for all true seekers, for those who work systematically, faithfully, with love. This is a new idea I am trying to give you of karma yoga. "*Maa phaleshu kadaachana*"—if you think of it in narrow terms, as a worker who works for eight hours and is not entitled to claim the wages of his work, it is the most stupid nonsense. I am always, nowadays, at variance with my great *acharyas* of the Hindu tradition because they have limited their interpretations to very narrow human ideals. They have not been able to elaborate beyond that. They have not been able to go beyond the human situation. In a sense, I think, they were not with the source, when they interpreted it.

So, for one who thinks of the ultimate goal of human life, the perfection that he has to achieve, these small intermediate goals of human endeavour have no meaning, should have no meaning. Otherwise the law says, "This you have got; this you shall keep, no more."

There are people who want small goals: happiness, good job, good husbands or good wives, or want to be free of sickness—yes surely you can achieve all these—it is too childish to talk about it, in a platform like Sahaj Marg. Some stupid nonsense of vitamins and carbohydrates and balanced food, and you have enough health; any fool can today make money. Any fool! If people don't make money, it is because they are lazy, not because they are not able to make money. They don't work. I mean, it would be silly to say you cannot make money nowadays when you see all the rich people around you. The standards of living, even in India, are rising. People who had to walk are now going around in bicycles and motorcycles. Even peasants don't walk; to go even one kilometre today they go by bus, they don't walk. Even to the most sacred religious temples in India, where tradition demands you walk, sometimes two thousand kilometres, they only reserve a small few hundred metres at the top, to have this ritualistic self-cheating, to say that, "I walked up the last few steps."

Prosperity has come in such large measure today, that we have lost sight of our original goal, the efforts that we are supposed to make, and therefore when we are asked to sit for meditation for half an hour, many of us say, "I cannot do it." If you cannot walk one kilometre, how are you going to sit in meditation? Please don't forget the law of opposites, which says, "He who does not work, cannot rest." He may want to rest, he may need rest, but he cannot rest! Precisely because, where there is no day, there cannot be a night and where there is no night, there cannot be a day either. It is like one of those dreams of science fiction, to imagine that if a planet stops rotating on its axis, one side will be day and one side will be night. It cannot stop. Because, like a toy of a child which is rotating and will remain stable only as long as it is rotating, and the moment it stops rotating on its own little nail, it will fall, no planet can be in orbit unless it is also rotating around itself. So, all these opposites we have not only to control, but we have to accept as necessary to our existence. Without good there is no evil; without evil there can be no good.

So if a society seeks to destroy all evil and retain only the good, it is doomed to failure from the start. Therefore the sanatana dharma says, "Don't make it so good that evil is also multiplying on the

25

other side." Where you build more temples, there are more brothels. Where there are more hospitals, there is more sickness. In a sense, it is the Peter Principle of management working, that "when you create a post, there is a manager ready to fill it." So sanatana dharma says, "Keep it at the minimum level." So that good is at the minimum and the bad is also at the minimum, and they balance very nicely. If you could go to one extreme in pleasure and good, you could go to the other extreme in pain and bad.

This is the great un-wisdom of Western societies, which are seeking to do good and to improve the standards of living of their people beyond all tolerable levels, so that misery is now proliferating, and which nobody can stop. How educated people can be so foolish is, for me, a permanent mystery. After all, whether because they are white or non-white, I don't know, most of the Nobel prizes go to the white-skinned. And yet they are destroying the world, with good intentions, to create a better society, to create a beautiful society, to create a nice society. And what have they done? You can see it for yourselves. Even if one white man has to run to the East, for anything whatsoever, that society is a failure. This is how I look at it.

Today we have this, for me a very nice and happy phenomenon, that we have more and more whites coming into the East, precisely because what they want, they cannot get there, not because there is some...*[break in tape]*...not just one or two or three. If there is the practice, and there are you, and there is the Master, but no link, well, you may

Master standing on the roof top of Library Building,
Manapakkam Ashram, Chennai

Master playing on the flute for abhyasis

achieve something very minimum. It is like a cart from which the horse has run away. Because of its own moment of inertia, it will move a few metres and stop. If there is the link, and you, and the Master, it is much better; if there is the link, and the practice, and the Master, but not you, it is stupid, it is hopeless. If there is the link, but no Master, there is you and the practice, again it is stupid, because without the Master, there is only a yoke to the cart. Nothing can pull it.

The ideal situation must be that "I am here." When I say, "I am here," I mean it in a different esoteric sense, that it is not enough that my body is here, but 'I' am in New York or 'I' am in Philadelphia, or 'I' am in Toronto or Montpellier. Most of us leave ourselves behind, and only the body comes here. We are at home celebrating *pongal* with the children or with the father-in-law who is going to berate us when we get back in the evening, or the mother-in-law waiting with a pair of spanners in her hands! So, where is the 'me' here? Where is the 'I' here?

Similarly, I may be here totally, but then my Master is not here with me and I think, "He is dead and gone. What shall I do?" The practice becomes just another exercise. So, 'I' must be here first; if I am not here, even my Master cannot help me, even my method cannot help me. The most important person for sadhana is 'me'. Having established that I am here, body and soul, I have to find the Master. Therefore, this 'I'-ness in a completely, integrated total form must be there right from the beginning, when you are even trying to find the Master, because if at that time, only the body is with the Master and you are at home, your choice can be wrong. So, I don't want to run over this point. You have all understood its main theme, that I am here, there is my Master, and the link between us—and this link is the most essential, because without the practice the link will take me with Him; but without the link, the practice can take me nowhere.

It is this link with the Master that is the most important thing, and the link must be a living link. With one whom we think is eternal, He cannot die, He can have no birth. If we limit Him to a temporary existence, than we limit ourselves, too, to a temporary existence because anything which applies to Him, must apply to me, too. Without His immortality, without His eternal existence, without His Ultimacy, I cannot aspire to live. A beggar cannot beg from another beggar. You can have a society of beggars, very nice, with office bearers, but they have to beg from somebody else. You can have the society of brahmins but they have to go to somebody else. You can have the society of *kshatriyas*, but they have to go to somebody else. Somebody says, "No, no, sir. I belong to the *kayasth* society." Yes, so what? Where will you go? You have to go to someone else, out of the society.

So, this is the great reason for breaking caste boundaries, career boundaries, national boundaries, temporal boundaries. If we don't break them, we shall be very much the slaves of that which we cannot break. It is like a prisoner in a cell. Either he must be let out or he must break out. None of us can break out of Fort Knox, for instance. So we need somebody to get us out. One who is inside the cell can rarely ever leave it by his own self effort, because cells are made to keep you there, not to let you out. If God made cells so easy, liberation would have been very easy millions of years back. Therefore wisdom says, "Find Him, who has to keep your sense. Invoke Him, love Him so much that He will come looking for you into the jail!" He will condescend to descend into the deepest dungeon where you are. He will be magnanimous enough to open the door. He will love you enough to catch hold of your hand and say, "Now come with me." So always we need someone. It must be the Master, because even for the smallest disease, if you have the best doctor, it is more of an assurance of health, than if you just say, "Oh, mine is a small sickness, let me find a small doctor." You don't go to a big restaurant when you are hungry and to a small restaurant when you are not so hungry. You find the best. So if that is the wisdom in ordinary matters, how much more should it be important to find the best Master available, the highest Master available?

Two days back I was talking about this, and I said, "Sahaj Marg is not Harvard, that we pick the best children of society and make them into good managers." Any fool could do that. I mean, if you could give me the best material available, I would turn out geniuses. Why only good managers? But the Master in Sahaj Marg, my Master, could take the worst and make it into the best. This is alchemy. We don't just make something better out of the poor atomicity. Here, there is a transmutation. There is a change of essence, like iron is made into coal, not into better iron, not into steel. Western technology is expert in that. You can take the poorest iron grade ore and make it into the best, beautiful white stainless steel—all the cutlery and crockery, which we feel like pinching when we travel by planes! I always have this urge to lift a few spoons and bring them home! They only make you more covetous. But in the East, the tradition has always been to make iron into gold—transmutation!

Therefore we find the people of the West coming here. They can make the same thing better; we can make the same thing into something else altogether different. The Western people are not fools to come to the East. If they only wanted to become better men, they have their own universities, centuries old, Edinburgh, Birmingham, what have you! But it is not enough. If a man is going to win a Nobel Prize and be a drug addict, that education will make him poor. That reward is not merited. And he who is the best, that man who gets the Nobel prize, must be having qualms of conscience: "What is it that they are giving me this prize, but I am still going for a shot of heroin in the street corner."

So, it is not an accident that people come to us here in the East. It is not an accident at all, because at least they are wise enough to know that what they are; if they became better in that, it is like a good thief becoming a better thief, becoming the best thief. No good! It is like an ordinary tubercular situation, becoming a very good tubercular situation, becoming the best tubercular situation, and dying.

Here we want change. Therefore Sahaj Marg stands for change, transmutation—not transformation, because in that there is only a change of form. Here, the essence is converted. As the Hindu *shastras* say, It is like making wine out of grape juice. The whole thing is changed; structurally it is changed; chemically it is changed. Its potability is different, its taste is different, and its effect is different.

So this is what Sahaj Marg stands for. This is what Sahaj Marg will achieve, provided, as I said, you are here. This ashram will serve us for the next several years, I hope, because eventually this is going to be a big campus, in which, I personally hope we shall be, able to celebrate Babuji Maharaj's birth centenary in the year 1999. We have no ambitious projects; we have only projects. We leave it to the divine will to complete it at its choice, in its time, in the way it wants. We have made a humble beginning. Such as it is we offer it to Him.

Thank you.

Evolution

Brothers and Sisters,

Ahmedabad is very fortunate in receiving, I think, about two hundred overseas abhyasis here. Some people were joking yesterday that we should transfer Basant celebrations to this place and I think we have already probably ten percent of the expected Basant attendance here. The important lesson we have to draw from this is the need to build our ashram here quickly because more and more people are going to come. There will be bigger attendance, more need for space, and more need for accommodation. I think in the years to come this land, which has always been the spiritual haven of this world, is going to attract more and more people. As they say, spiritual refugees! It is going to be the land of the virtuous. There are quite considerable apprehensions for the future trend of the world. But this may not afford a material haven, but a spiritual place of refuge, which India will certainly always be.

So when we are thinking of more facilities available, it is also to cater to that future need which we have to anticipate even now. It is not an accident that more and more people are joining the Mission, trying to come to the spiritual fold, because as the world is exploding towards material satiation, side by side comes the realisation that material values

Talk at Ahmedabad on 28 January, 1990

are just like dust and ashes. More and more of a good thing doesn't make better things. One can eat only so much of chocolate and ice creams. Then comes the inevitable disenchantment, disillusionment with the material life. More and more powerful cars, better clothes, better cosmetics—there is a limit. The inner urge cannot be stifled; it's like a volcano. The wise recognise the presence of the inner urge and start a spiritual life quickly, the not so wise wait for the explosive forces to gather inside, and then comes some time when there is no other choice.

I personally believe that they should choose the spiritual life out of a wise knowledge of the real values of existence, rather than be pushed into it by a disenchantment and disillusionment and frustration with the material life. What happens today is more and more in that spirit; that is why we find more and more young people coming. They are now wise, wiser than the old, because they see the frustration of the elder generation. They see their mistakes, they see their suffering, they see their sorrows, and are able to draw the lesson that, "What they have done, we should not do; what they have not done, we should do." It is not an accident that we get more young people. It has always been felt, even in the Vedas, that "the son is the father of man." A son can never be the father of man in the physical sense. But they are definitely the wiser, and we hope that the future generations will be yet wiser, so that again we will have those famous prodigies of spirituality like Markandeya and

Dhruva, child prodigies, like Lava and Kusha. Now they only are names.

In the Hindu families we are very famous for having the names of these famous progenitors of our race, without following their precepts, without following their examples. But a time is coming that we will follow not only the examples but also achieve what they achieved. Prodigies are always children; nobody talks of a seventy-year-old prodigy. It's not an accident that prodigies are always children and the younger they are, the greater they are. If a child can play a virtuoso performance on the piano table, that is a prodigy. At the age of seventy-two, he may be the best pianist in the world, but he is not a prodigy.

So, it is towards prodigies that we look. That is the promise of the future, that the sooner we are able to aspire for and achieve the spiritual existence, the sooner this land, this world, will be blessed by a spiritual fulfilment of the inner verities of life, without which we are only going towards insane destruction. The search for pleasure is always fraught with destructive endings. Pleasure must end in pain; it can have no other ending. So when we look for pleasure, it is a inevitable that our life will end with pain, with sorrow, with misery, with frustration. When we look for growth, when we look for evolution, there comes a fulfilment. It may not be pleasure, it may not even be satisfaction, but it is a growth. It is an evolutionary thing. And there is a fulfilment in it: a fulfilment of spirit, a fulfilment of the heart, which you cannot duplicate in the material existence.

These are the things which Sahaj Marg offers. Sahaj Marg does not offer a materially satisfactory life. If by your past samskara, you have also earned a materially satisfactory life, you can consider that to be an added blessing. But the way of the spirit has always been one with the way of material poverty. It does not mean we are beggars. We impoverish ourselves by doing away with all unwanted things, throwing off unnecessary things, tearing down our material existence to the barest minimum fulfilment of needs.

So we don't have this modern disease, I should say, the shackles of the modern executive, where people have to run around looking for more and more work and more and more time to do that work, neglecting the spiritual life and saying, "I have no time for it." They have no time for meditation. This is a modern disease. It's like saying, "I have no time to live." Well, one who has no time to live is surely going to die; one who has no time for spirituality is bound to die a material life. And therefore he becomes grosser and grosser and you get into the downward trend of materialisation, when eventually you shall end up so gross that perhaps it is a mineral life, a rock-like life. These are not some sort of divine dispensations that are forced upon us. These are inevitable tendencies with which, if you co-operate, you end up with the fulfilment of that particular tendency. Where it is too cold, water has to freeze and become ice. If it is not heated again, if it is not warmed again it will remain ice even for eternity. You do not have to look very far, you only have to go to the northern regions of the world to find what they call regions of perpetual snow, perpetual ice, which nothing could melt.

So that is the danger of the material civilisation and the material individual life, that we become so solid that nothing can unsolidify us again. I think it is for this reason that the great souls whom we call Masters come again and again to teach us *tapa*, from which the word *tapasya* comes, so that by their spiritual heat, by their spiritual truths of life, they add some warmth to this eternally cold life that we have inherited from our own past, created from our own past, and we get a new chance.

We just move on from there and, if you miss that chance, as Babuji says, you will have to wait several thousand years again.

So such periods of spiritual availability, spiritual possibility, are small and rather short interregnums in a vast era of pains and miseries. Those who are wise will recognise that we are here not by an accident of nature but because of some samskara that we have earned, our good nature which has got us onto this planet at the right time, in the right company of that great person who is our Master. If we miss this boat, we will have to wait for the next boat. In India you are all familiar with late trains, missed trains, missed planes; how much we suffer when we miss a plane. How much turmoil of the heart, impatience of the heart to reach your destination for a few mere hours of missed opportunity. But that wisdom we don't translate into the missed opportunity of a spiritual life. And then when we are bound down to this earth by the gravity of our own grossness, life after life, with nothing to help us, sinking deeper and deeper into that heaviness of an existence of materiality, who can we curse but ourselves?

So you see, it is not something that you can miss today and accept tomorrow again. Opportunities missed may not recur, you see. Spiritual life is not like a running train, or a plane; there is some guarantee that is you miss one plane another one will come, if not today, tomorrow; if not tomorrow, next week. We have the time, because days don't matter much in a life span of, say, eighty years. But, if you take the birth of a great saint, a great personality, who can offer us liberation with what Babuji calls the blink of an eye, and if such a personality comes once in five thousand years, then we have no choice. If you miss this bus, the next bus may be after fifty lifetimes. And then, too, only if you are fortunate enough to be born with Him. And He should be accessible to us, and we should be accessible to Him.

Now many of these disabilities of the past we have overcome by this enormous, what shall we say, grace, compassion of the Master who makes transmission possible over undefined lengths of time and space. But even that will not last forever. It can only be during the Master's lifetime. This chain must be kept perpetually alive—to that also we have to co-operate. So, I am only trying to impress upon you the seriousness of our meetings, how they offer an opportunity for a spiritual renewal from inside, how that opportunity, if missed—we may think it is not a big tragedy. After all, there will be another sitting this evening; there will be one more tomorrow; there is Basant next week at Bombay. Yes! But you remember the famous English proverb that "betwixt that between the cup and the lip there is many a slip." We must always remember that human life is a very frail existence. That it doesn't take much to just knock out this life, like blowing out a candle. There is no guarantee that we will be here for the next Basant, and the next after that.

So we must remember Babuji's advice, that a wise man is one who lives as if he is going to die the next moment. This is the ultimate wisdom: not to depend on the continuity of life, as if it is going to give me a perpetual chance which I can miss today and can grasp again tomorrow. Because you know how habits are formed—what you do today, you do will better tomorrow; what you miss today; you will miss better tomorrow; the day after tomorrow you will miss it even more. One who cannot wake up today will not wake up tomorrow at all; one who will not sit in meditation today will find it more difficult tomorrow, and much more difficult the day after.

The secret of success in meditation is to do it so well that it becomes a habit, and eventually it becomes a way of life, without which we cannot exist. We must feel uneasy if we don't have the morning meditation. So uneasy that you convert it into the first activity of your daily life: wake up and meditate. Now, you see, people want their morning cup of tea and their morning cup of coffee, without which nothing moves, physically and in other ways. Why not we should take it also the motive force behind our existence itself? Without meditation I cannot exist. There must be a restlessness, a craving, that the moment I wake up I do meditation. Then goes on the rest of the activity. It should not be something done under compulsion, under duress, under even fear; it must become as natural as breathing.

I believe that is also a way in which we can consider constant remembrance. If I am to remember consciously every moment and say, "Yes I remember Babuji, I remember Babuji," it is no more constant remembrance. It is a forced remembrance. It is like the breathing of a patient with a heart problem, who has to breathe consciously, or is conscious of every breath that he takes. Such a life is doomed. Because if he forgets to breathe, he is dead. So we have to breathe in such a way that we are not even conscious that we are breathing. Our heart must function in such a way that we are not conscious of its functioning. Our digestion must go on in such a way that we are not conscious of our digestion. You know, consciousness of the functions means a derangement. Meditation, too, must become like that, something so automatic, so natural, so spontaneous, so vital to our existence that we go on without conscious effort. Then it becomes possible to say, such a person is always in meditation, though always consciously involved in his other aspects of existence. Then he is in constant remembrance. Meditation, constant remembrance, all become one activity. It is towards this aim that all our meditative practices are focussed. This is why this necessitates or requires regular meditation, conscious participation at fixed times, in a fixed place, so that it becomes a habit and then it becomes something in which you involve yourself without even knowing it, so that eventually there is a person who is meditating all the time, who is in constant remembrance all the time and yet able to do everything that life demands of us in the material world, without that having any effects upon us. At that stage it becomes possible to say, he lives without forming impressions, therefore there are no more samskaras. Such a person is liberated.

This is a short sort of sketch of what Sahaj Marg is all about and, as I said, we in India especially have a sacred trust, that we keep this lamp as a safe spiritual refuge for posterity. Every bit of this country is sacred in this respect. Every square inch of India has been bearing the footprints of the great sages of the past. Nowhere in India you will find a place where there has not been a saint or saints who has not walked that land, who has not meditated, who has not done *tapasya*. But like all great things, it is not for us alone; it is for everybody in this world. So in that sense we Indians are trustees for this sacred heritage, the sacred spiritual wealth that India has always offered, and will always continue to offer, to the world. In that spirit we invite all our brothers and sisters from abroad and, of course, our own brothers and sisters who are still too ignorant to realise the value of what they are sitting upon themselves. They are very much like chicken sitting on an egg out of some inner compulsion and nature, not knowing that that egg bears the next generation of its own kind. It is like a man who is sleeping on a gold mine and begging for his food outside. It is like a man whose father has buried a pot-full of diamonds under his pillow, and he is sleeping on it and having dreams of poverty and disease and misery. Dig it! And you find here they have to dig in their heart; this is our gold mine; this is our diamond mine. This is mine in which God exists; it is a mine of God.

I pray on this occasion that Babuji may bless all of you with these spiritual achievements for yourself and for the future, and make you all conscious that you are not only here for yourself but as trustees for the future, and I pray for His blessings.

Thank you.

Basant Message

The annual celebration of the Birth Anniversary of our Adi Guru, Param Pujya Lalaji Maharaj Saheb, represents the passing of yet another 'year-stone' in our existence. I have called it a year-stone, you can call it a time-stone, like a space-stone. You have milestones, kilometre stones; I consider a month and a year to be stones which mark the passage of time. So I have called it another year-stone in our existence. It dramatises the passing of yet another year. While we are gathering to celebrate the auspicious occasion of his Birth Anniversary, it is also necessary to take stock of one's own spiritual progress and evolution, and to see whether a mile-stone has also been passed on the spiritual path which we are treading towards our Goal.

The idea is that we get old without any effort on our part. Time moves inexorably, as they say. Nothing is necessary; we can just relax in our easy chairs and keep going older and older. Unless death takes a hand in between. So it is a hint that to grow old doesn't require any effort. Everybody gets old. Fools get old; wise get old; saints get old; sinners get old; mountains get old; stones get old. What is their merit in getting old? In our country there is a respect for the aged people. I think we should respect the aged not because they are aged, but because they have had a successful battle with

Talk given at Bombay on 31 January, 1990

death longer than others have had. To that extent perhaps they merit some consideration or respect, but unless they have also aged in their progress— like the French people have their wines which mature. They grow old and they grow also beautiful in quality, according to the French people. But suppose the old is sourer than the young wine, nobody would drink it.

So it is the duty of the aged or it is our duty as we grow older and older to also mature with that growth. This is the idea that I have tried to give. Year-stones inevitably pass by because the passage of time is inexorable. Passing mile-stones depends on the speed with which we progress on the path towards the Goal. The idea is fairly clear.

It is a common human failing to mistake year-stones for mile-stones, and to rest content with the feeling that all is well, imagining that one more Basant has been celebrated, one more celebration of my Revered Master's Birth Anniversary has been celebrated, and to think that therefore we have been recipients of the Divine flow of grace.

It is true that grace is available to all who seek it. To seek means to search. And to search in the Sahaj Marg tradition is to go within. How successful have we been in going inwards towards the destination which, after all, lies deep within ourselves? This is a question we should ask ourselves every day. The idea behind writing the diary is precisely this, because when you want to write a diary, you have to think what happened that day, what happened during meditation, what happened after meditation? Have there been changes which you have perceived? Which means searching within yourself for possible clues of any change in our character, in our behaviour, in ourselves. It is pertinent to ponder over this question, because if one is going outwards all the time in his or her normal existence, then even if such a person is meditating for the stipulated period of time, it may possibly be that he has not been successful in going inwards in the spiritual tradition. The essence, indeed the crux of the matter, is this internal voyage. And it can be successful only to the extent that we stop external probing in the sensory and other aspects of our day to day lives.

There is much talk of God, the Master, among the abhyasis. I am of the opinion that when normally God or the Master is referred to, by and large, the abhyasis are still in the same frame of mind as when they were following the religious tradition or other traditions, i.e., they think of God or the Master as being somewhere far away, towards whom they have to physically move to achieve the goal that is offered in Sahaj Marg. This is a very common observation, that we think of Master somewhere, ourselves somewhere, and the impunity with which many people break laws is a testament to this inner belief that God is not there at all for Him to see what is happening.

We are convenient moralists, or the idea that God is somewhere, or the Master is somewhere and we are here is a convenience which the mind adopts, because then he is not a direct witness to our mistakes. Temple worship, as I have often said in the past, is a very convenient system for this. We can do what we have to at our homes, blindly imagining that God is blind; He cannot see what we are doing, He has no *doordarshan* facility available to him. Therefore when we do all these things and when the burden we impose upon ourselves becomes too large, sometimes we go to a temple, put a hundred rupees in the *hundi,* thinking that all that has been wiped out. We leave God where He is, because then we are free to do what we can at home, what we have to at home, what we must, in the wrong ways.

It is my experience, and my conviction arising out of the experience that God or the Master—both terms are synonymous for me—have no location in space and no existence in time, because the Master is not, and cannot be, bound by either space or time. It is a well-known truth that anything which has spatial dimensions must cease to exist at some point in time. This only means that anything having a spatial existence is also automatically bound by the time dimension, that is, it has a definite life period.

It is, therefore, obvious that to possess the attribute of eternity one must be non-space-bound and non-time-bound, too. One cannot conceive of such a situation with the normal, rational apparatus of the intellect. But by meditation, which teaches us to look inwards within ourselves, one is able to internally intuit at what the Master or God must be. Such a person, or such an individual, must have transcended both the space and time dimensions, because eternity is not an extension in time. It is not even infinite time, but it is an aspect of eternity. As one cannot conquer space, or transcend space, by traversing the vast physical reaches of this universe, which in any case is impossible within the lifetime of a human being, similarly eternity cannot be thought of as an infinite extension of the time dimension.

I believe that, as we exist in space, and all space is the same, the only way of transcending space is to go beyond space. Similarly, existing in time, we have to transcend time and get approach to the infinite, which we call eternity. I personally believe that this is possible only by going inwards and inwards, and yet inwards, until we become the Being with no space dimension and therefore no time dimension, too. Because, after all, time and space are mutually inter-dependent. It is for this reason that the Master cannot be located in physical space nor in temporal time but, being beyond both, having transcended both, is one having His existence in a timeless, space-less eternity. Of such a Being alone can it be said, "He neither exists nor is He non-existent!" This is the famous refrain from the Vedas, the *nasadiya sukta* of which Babuji is so fond. He has quoted it again and again. It neither is, nor is not. So it is something in between.

You cannot say of God that He exists. Where is He? You cannot say that He is non-existent because everything that you see around testifies to His Presence. So He is something in between. Such a person is invulnerable, precisely for this reason that He cannot be located either in space or in time. This is by the way. He whom you cannot approach either in space or time, you cannot touch, you cannot see, you cannot feel. The only way to approach such a One is for us similarly to follow the path that He has trod, and to achieve the same state of Being as His. In this process we will become endowed with the eternal existence and then, the two being one, there is a fusionless-fusion, which we call the *layavastha* in Sahaj Marg terminology.

I would like to mention here that when we talk of *laya*, we have this common cinema idea that two people come and become one—even in our mythological stories of the great saints, who just fall at the feet of some Lord in the temple and you see the soul going into it. I don't think *laya* is any such thing. *Laya* is just like the breeze in the room becomes the breeze outside the room. You cannot distinguish which was and which is and which merged together. That is my idea. Maybe it is right, maybe it is wrong.

To go inwards is the sole purpose of our being, because this alone can endow us with the spiritual being which is our goal. Meditation is the only way. Co-operation by way of not allowing ourselves to spread outwards in the internal aspects of life is the essential aspect of sadhana. Sadhana is not just doing our meditation and our cleaning and our night-time prayer. Sadhana also means not going outwards into unnecessary physical activities of our life, not becoming too much involved in business, not become too much attached to our offices, not too much attached to money. Because otherwise you are pulling this way, that is pulling this way, and we are lost.

So we have to go out into meditation and draw in our daily activities. It is a dual approach that we have to adopt because if one alone is there, it is of no use. It is often a failure. Then the operation of these two factors will bless the abhyasi with approach to the goal. Otherwise success will surely elude a *sadhaka*, though by the Master's grace, he may have some crumbs falling to his share from the Master's table.

I pray that all may develop the wisdom and the fortitude necessary to pursue the path of evolution with single minded purpose in this way, so that the goal can be easily achieved. May it be so, by His grace and blessings.

A New Vision

I had an experience I never had before. Of course, one of the extraordinary things is that there are almost five thousand abhyasis present here. We have a record overseas attendance of almost three hundred, and yesterday in the preceptors' meeting we had about two hundred and sixty preceptors. All these are, of course, extraordinary facts.

I remember when I first attended Basant in 1965, the total area of our *shamiyana* was the *chabutra* in Babuji's house. It was like that for many years. I think there were forty-two people totally present and the Working Committee was composed of all the preceptors in those days, and there were eleven preceptors. And to bring those eleven people together sometimes took us one day, because they were going in all directions. And Babuji was very formal and sometimes quite concerned about what the Working Committee would do and how they would deliberate and what they would speak. It was almost always a very charged atmosphere in those days.

Forty-two people, and I remember, it used to take us three hours to eat, because in that same chabutra we had to have meditation, then we had to have talks, then twelve or thirteen at a time we would be fed in three or four batches. By the time we went to bed it was one o'clock at night. We would

---

Talk at Bombay on 1st February, 1990.

wake up at 3:30 in the morning so that we could go to the toilet first, have our bath, and come first. Very exciting days! Very emotional days full of spiritual charge. A very small group and it was not very wonderful or very surprising that we were all very close to Master, because there He used to sit in the veranda just near the pillar and some thirty or forty of us around him, like his children and grand-children. And there to get a place, we would go and have our bath at half past three and sit right in front of his chair, because 6:30 was always meditation. And at 6:15 somebody would have to go to the toilet again, and he would miss his place! We had to sit on the cold floor with just one *dhari* like this and we used to tuck ourselves with blankets, cover our ears, cover our nose, so that even the wisp, slightest wisp of air, should not penetrate, and as the French say, *voila*, suddenly you have to go to the toilet, you not only miss your place, you miss the comfort. And in those forty people there was always a jockeying for position.

I used to wonder what it would be like when it became few hundreds. That, we saw in the next four or five years. I think by 1968 we had to take the *Khatri Dharmasala*, when we had a couple of hundred people. And then Babuji's house, the whole chabutra, all the rooms used to be packed. We used to sleep on the floor with some hay, spread very thin, just freshly cut. Some sort of insulation! Because the cement floors were very cold. We used to bathe in cold water. There was no question of hot water.

They were wonderful days and I never thought we would see such wonderful days again. Honestly, because it was such a close intimate circle. Forty people, fifty people, hundred people. It is always my regret that in the days after those years up to 1968 or 1969, the Master became more and more remote from his abhyasis in a physical sense. Because soon, I think by 1974, we already had touched a thousand abhyasis for Basant. By the time the ashram was opened, it was almost fifteen hundred. For Lalaji's birth centenary in Madras in 1973, we already had fourteen or fifteen hundred people present. And as more and more people started coming, of course, the individual experiences during the sittings were always full of remarkable experiences.

This was what served to maintain the intimate link between the Master and his abhyasis. Because the day soon came when somebody is sitting, say, a hundred metres or two hundred metres away, and many people could not have personal touch with Babuji, my Master. It was always my concern that this intimacy, which was originally physical and very closely personal, should be preserved at all cost. And, of course, it was apparent that it could only happen in a spiritual way, because today we are five thousand here and it is not possible to meet everyone individually.

So what was the remarkable thing about today's experience? Today's experience, I felt two things. That was on the Basant morning, 31st morning meditation. I felt as if all the abhyasis were with me here. It was not a question of, they are

51

small like ants and all sitting in front of me. It was as if we were all on this one stage. And soon after I felt, for the first time, the presence of Lord Krishna, next to Him, Lord Lalaji Maharaj, next to Him, Lord Babuji Maharaj, all three standing behind me.

Now Babuji's presence we frequently feel. He is, after all, our Master and it is his business to be with us. Lalaji Maharaj's presence is much rarer. Lord Krishna's vision I have had in some experiences during meditation with Babuji and with Sister Kasturi. They were visions; I could not say whether it was a presence or not. This was the first occasion on which I felt the Lord of *Yuga*, *Mahapurusha* of *Yuga* and the controller of the universe and His Master, all three behind us. So I think there is something very fundamental and something unique and something remarkable going to happen to this Mission. The future, if I may say so,. is blessed by this triumvirate of Sahaj Marg. Lord Krishna's picture we don't keep, because He is not only our Master, but He is the Master of the universe. But He is there. Without Him there is no *yuga*, there is no universe, no *srishti*. The *Kali Yuga* is His.

So this is something I wanted to share with you and to tell you, how unique these occasions can be. How personal, how intimate, how close our connection can be, not withstanding a separate, I mean, a physical distance between us, a separation physically between us. There is no need to feel either the need for detachment or the need to be sorrowful that we cannot meet as we used to meet in the old days, because His Grace, His presence ensures that, physically separate though we may be, spiritually we are linked, perhaps forever. If we look to the past, we know we have been with the Master, at least I have been told that I was his disciple in another life, two lives. Backwards we can see the way; forwards, we cannot see the way. Therefore, we have to draw certain conclusions from looking back. You know, like when you climb a mountain, if you see the road below you, you say that is the way I came, but the road up is not so clear. Then we become lonely, we become frightened, we become, concerned. "It is getting dark, how will I go up?" Well we have come so far. When we were there, this road also looked bleak and forbidding and dark. But we have nevertheless come so far. Why should we imagine that He who has brought us so far will not take us further until the end?

So these are the conclusions, these are the feelings, you see, very personal, very real feelings that have come up during this, what should I say, very glorious celebration of Lalaji Maharaj's birth anniversary which gives, at least to me personally, enormous confidence and tremendous courage to face the future, whatever it may be. Now the future will contain everything. Like the past has contained everything, the future too will contain everything. There cannot be a future with only one single content in it. That will be only when we reach our destination.

So it only means that we cannot be selective in our approach to the future, we cannot demand of the Master that my future shall be this and this and this. The road may be one, but the terrain will

53

change; there will be mountains, there will be valleys, there will be rivers to cross, precipices to jump over perhaps, rivers to wade through where there are no bridges.

We cannot demand an easy path. But we can surely depend upon the guidance that is available to us, whose judgement is absolute, whose love is absolute, whose generosity is total, whose commitment to our progress is also absolute. I have always felt a sense of commitment to all of you—not because Babuji told me I am committed to this—but because in his book, I think in *Voice Real*, he says: "There shall certainly be one after me who shall give you the same service as I have done." That puts upon me a sense of commitment more than anything he could have said himself. He never said, "Parthasarathi you have to do what I have done." He always said, "You will do what I have done." In fact, He told me, "Under you, the Mission will shine much brighter than I could ever make it shine because the time for it is there, because Lalaji's wish is like that, because it is the demand of the time, because it is the way Nature wants it, because it is Nature's plan."

So all that we do is to make the ultimate plan of the ultimate Master, God Himself, through His representatives, unroll before us, like unrolling a carpet. And we must have the humility, the love, and the courage to see what unfolds before us is what He wishes to unfold before us. We have no right to be selective in our approach to the future. What He wishes is my wish; what he wants for me, is what I want. What He has desired for me should be my desire; what He sets before me as my goal should be my goal. And when He is with me, we should be like children walking with their parents, unconcerned.

I hope that all abhyasis will develop this confidence of a child in its parent, just holding the little finger of the father or the mother's hand, and walking and dancing and singing on the street. It has no concern for the road, it has no concern for the traffic, it has no concern for where it is going. But it is blithe of spirit, joyful of heart, content to be with them whom it loves.

I would like to suggest that the spiritual journey should be like that, not even the idea of a destination should bother us, not even the idea of a goal should concern us because then, there is always this problem: "Will the Master be with me till I reach the Goal?" There have been instances in all our lives when we are going on the road and someone comes with us up to a certain point and says, "Now *bhaisaab*, you go that way, I am going this way." Then we have to seek a fresh companion. You see, human companionship changes. Some are there with us for a few days, some are there with us for a few years. No human companionship lasts in any case beyond your lifetime. But, it is said that the spiritual companionship of the Master can be eternal if you choose to make it so. It **can** be eternal. Whether it will be, depends on you, each one of you. How to make it eternal? By holding on to Him in such a way that either He cannot leave us nor can we leave Him. Babuji Maharaj always said, "I can

55

never cut myself off from you, but if you are wilful enough to do it, you can cut yourself off from me."

You see, that is the absolute generosity and the freedom of Nature, that at no time will it bind you against your will to itself in the form of the Master. He is there always; He is there always available; He is there waiting for us. It is for us to hold His hand and not to let go.

So, I would request that people, abhyasis, remember that the connection and the strength of the connection is something we have to create. And if you say, "The Master must do that, too," it will be very stupid. I have often heard abhyasis talk very slightingly of Sahaj Marg. Even this morning I was sorry when one abhyasi said, "I had almost left Sahaj Marg," for some reason. Now how can an abhyasi talk like this? How can we ever think of leaving Sahaj Marg? Is there something other than Sahaj Marg for us? If you are going by train from here to Lucknow, there is a train for you. You cannot say, "This is uncomfortable. I will get out," and, "This is uncomfortable. I will walk out." If you walk out, you are on the station, in the middle of the night, not knowing where the next train will come up, at the mercy of the people there, not knowing where to sleep, where to go, what you will do next.

I hope and pray sincerely that no abhyasi will ever utter these disgraceful words that, "I shall leave Sahaj Marg," or "I want to leave Sahaj Marg." Because believe me, outside Sahaj Marg there is only the darkness, there is the filth, there is the criminality of the world.

You may not prosper very well in this way, but prosper you will. How well you will prosper depends on you. How soon you will walk with the Master depends on the speed with which you can walk. Because His speed is always matched to your speed. It is, again, the love of a parent. When you have a child who is one year old, you take him and walk at his speed. You don't pull him along. When he is three, he is able to walk a little faster, and you walk a little faster. When he is eighteen, you walk shoulder to shoulder, arms swinging at seven miles an hour, let us say. The Master's speed can be infinite. If Lalaji Maharaj was able to do it in seven months without even the benefit of a real guru's guidance, I don't see why we should not do it in seven years. I told Babuji Maharaj once, "Why do you think only Lalaji should have been capable? Do you think we are any less?" He said, "No, it is not like that, but nobody had that single-mindedness of purpose which he had, you see." If you have that, why seven months? Maybe in seven days it should be possible. After all, in these things, when Babuji Maharaj said, "Turn your head from here to here and there He is," it should only take a second. So you see, how long it takes depends on upon us; how far we shall go depends upon us.

The responsibility cast upon the abhyasi in Sahaj Marg is a total responsibility. Not for sadhana, not for meditation, not for constant remembrance. All these are, shall I say, subordinate elements of our connection with the Master. But for the true connection which must be eternally there between us, that of an association of love about which I

57

spoke this morning. It is love which makes us hold another person's hand, not faith. Faith is a smaller thing. Not confidence, that is even less, because at a moment we may lose confidence and let go. For instance, if you have to jump a gap of sixteen feet and he says, "Hold my hand and jump with me," he may jump. I may let go and I will fall into the ravine. It takes enormous courage to hold the hand of a man who is going like that, in leaps and bounds.

Therefore in His mercy, He walks at our pace, and then we blame Him for going so slowly! "What is this, Babuji, you are going so slowly." He says, "Yes, my son. I am old, you know." Even then, he doesn't want to blame us, that it is your pace which is hindering me.

So, if you want to really test the Master and how fast He can walk on this road to freedom, to liberty, to the ultimate, try running on it. Try the marathon. How long can He walk? Try it. And then you will find that, that old man who could only walk at say, two metres per hour with a child, can also walk two million kilometres in that same time, if you have the ability to do it. Therefore, whenever we question the Master's ability to help us, it is a reflection of our ability to walk with Him, to sit with Him, to speak with Him, to understand Him.

Please remember that He is the mirror, and if you see the image walking slowly, it means you, the object, are walking slowly. So, in Sahaj Marg our progress depends on us. His help is always there. His hand is ever held out, in help, in guidance for us to grasp. So I would like abhyasis to feel a sense of commitment. Not to the Mission, the Mission is only an organisation; not the method, because the method is also something created for us to understand and assimilate all the principles which must govern our association with the Master. We must feel a sense of commitment to Him. He is mine, He expects so much of me, not for His sake but for our sake. It is like a father who wants his son to be successful in school, successful in college, successful in his life, not for himself but for the son's sake. And if we feel the sense of commitment to Him and His expectations of us for our sakes, our journey will become very quick, it will become very easy. We shall be there even before we know that we have left this place.

This is the immense possibility that lies before us in Sahaj Marg. But if we deal with it in a trivial way, in a materialist way, thinking of it as a Mission and a Master and a method, and the elements of *pooja*, and *dhyana*, and meditation, and cleaning, and all these things, then it is like dealing with a bowl of rice and counting the grains of rice. This is *dhal*, this is rice, this is something else—we get lost. It is like that old saying, "losing the forest for the trees." We have to learn to look upon Sahaj Marg with a new vision, the totality, that Sahaj Marg is the Master, our goal is the Master, our guide is the Master. Our purpose is to become like the Master. Then the emphasis on the Master all the time, and if we are able to do this, there shall surely be success in the shortest possible time, for which I pray for all of you.

Thank you.

Prayer

This nine o'clock prayer, I first read about in Babuji's *Voice Real*. I had to print the book, so when I was reading it, I saw about it. I asked Babuji, "Why you didn't tell me about this?"

He said, " I have stopped it."

I said, "Why?"

He said, "Because nobody does it."

What is the use of propagating something which nobody will do? So Babuji Maharaj wanted so many things to be done. I think, in the beginning his teaching must have been very wide. I have complete faith and conviction in this. But many things he dropped because people were not doing. Everybody knows that meditation was for one hour and he reduced it to half an hour because people refused to meditate for one hour. Similarly evening prayer, he said ten minutes. Originally it should have been half an hour. Cleaning should have been half an hour.

So in his effort to get us to do something, he dropped many items of sadhana from the original course. This is my absolute conviction. I have heard from him so often with this very idea. In fact, if you have read some of my books dealing with his overseas travels, in Germany he said he would stop printing books altogether because he said, "Nobody reads them." What is the use of printing books which nobody reads?

I remember it was in Delhi, just before we left for the 1976 tour. Babuji thought one particular article which had appeared in the *Sahaj Marg Patrika* was very important. Two preceptors came. Babuji was talking about this, and they immediately, without keeping quiet, said, "Babuji, in which book has this been printed?" He said, "It is in the *Patrika* of this month. Have you not read it?" And he was quite upset! He said, "These are preceptors!" Preceptors should read more than abhyasis. They should read all the Mission literature so that they can talk about it to abhyasis.

That is why it was something of a heart-break for my Master that he found preceptors giving wrong advice to abhyasis, wrong teaching to abhyasis, talking nonsense, virtually. That is why at one particular stage, I think it was in 1976, he wrote me a letter saying, "Both of us should stop making preceptors." This letter has been made much of by the opposite camp who pretend that it is a letter withdrawing my powers to make preceptors. But the fact is, the letter specifically says, "We should stop making preceptors now. Because, preceptors are there; they are not working; they are not reading; they are not teaching properly; they don't themselves meditate."

So this nine o'clock prayer is not something I have introduced. It is part of the Sahaj Marg sadhana *paddhati*. Now it was dropped! I think it is time to give ourselves a chance to make use of the original *angas* of Sahaj Marg for our benefit and for everybody's benefit.

When the walls of communism started crumbling a few months ago, and totalitarian states were compelled to open their boundaries, their borders allowing free flow of people, ideas, materials, the whole of humanity heaved a sigh of relief. Not because our European brothers on the other side of the borders are great humanitarians, but because when there is a threat to freedom even in a small pocket, that disease can spread everywhere else. When there is totalitarianism and weaponry of the ultimate destructive nature in one part of the world, it is a potential threat to the rest of the world.

Freedom means freedom from fear, fundamentally. All these French ideas of freedom, that we should be able to walk on the streets, drinking what we want, that is stupid. Real freedom is freedom from fear, not in freedom of movement, not in freedom to shake hands with whom you like. So long as there is fear there can be no freedom. This is true freedom. Freedom from freedom means freedom from the fear. So, when totalitarian states vanished overnight, as it were, and boundaries were open and champagne was drunk, the world was relieved that what was potentially a disease pocket, is now going, by the grace of the Almighty.

Now this could not have been possible unless these pockets of resistance, of disease, of potential menace of possible world destruction, the people across the border have looked upon them as brothers. If, to the West German, the East German was something to be sneered at, a lesser form of humanity, stupid, crazy, downtrodden, there would not have been this surge of happiness when they regained their relative freedom.

Now, regarding the nine o'clock prayer, one thing I should like to emphasise: In Sahaj Marg we are always thinking of creating a brotherhood. If we have to look upon Babuji's teachings with perspicacity and wisdom, you start to think of someone as a brother, only when you have not thought of him as a brother before. So, this means all along we are thinking of other races as different, as something below our attention, as something not to be loved but only to be exploited—they are black, they are yellow, they are blue, they are green, they are stupid. We need to create, but when we sit in this nine o'clock prayer, and view humanity as one unit: "They are already my brothers and sisters. Let their hearts be filled with the same love which is filling my heart; let their hearts shine with that faith which is trying to illuminate my heart; let them aspire for that goal for which I am aspiring." What brother Durai said about Swami Vivekananda—"I have found Him." Vivekananda had the generosity, the magnanimity, the love for humanity, that he could cross several oceans without a penny in his pocket, and in his saffron robes, braving the cold of Chicago, he could stand up and address that enormous multitude of people there in the Parliament of Religions, and address them as "Sisters and brothers of America." It was not the rest of the speech which made him so great, it was that cry of his heart which said, "Sisters and brothers of America." No American had felt that he had sisters and brothers before; there were only girls and boys, men and women, exploited and exploiting.

It was that single phrase, this is my intuition, you see, the rest of it is spiritual blah-blah. Everybody knows about it. Who had the courage to address them as sisters and brothers? And, I am from Asia, the dirty Indian, standing up, facing the white man, and saying "Sisters and brothers"—that was a lion's roar, not just a spiritual talk! We have to think that they are sisters and brothers because we are one, we are human beings. And when we think of somebody that they are **going** to be my brothers and sisters, we have created a barrier. We must remember what Babuji has said, when some people asked him, "How to make non-abhyasis into abhyasis," he said, "Why do you think they are non-abhyasis?" Let **them** think. Because if you, as a preceptor, think they are non-abhyasis, they will remain non-abhyasis.

So, you see, the thought of the human being is of the highest subtlety. It partakes of the divine power of whatever it is, thinking, thought, thought-content. So, if you are just thinking, "Let this man be my brother," you have already divided him, away from you, separated, and now the process that you are going to adopt to bring him nearer, perhaps may send him farther away. It is well-known that if you give charity in an ostentatious manner, it ceases to be charity; it makes of the recipient a beggar. All this greatness attributed to Jesus Christ—"Let not thy right hand know what thy left hand is doing"—is for two purposes: When you give ostentatiously, you make the other man squirm under your generosity, under your friendship. He hates you for it. And if your left hand knows what your right hand is doing, which means that I know that I am giving someone something, it makes the giver arrogant, prideful, boastful—"I have helped so and so." It harms two people at once, the giver and the receiver.

This is what Babuji meant when he talked of "social service." "What social service?" he said. "Feeding the poor people, giving them clothes! This is your duty for your brothers and sisters. Don't make a big *tamasha* and a show off, and you build buildings to charity, putting your names on them. This is arrogance, this is pride. It will not help the receiver. It will not help you at all, the giver."

Recently one day I was walking and I had a short talk with some of our overseas abhyasis about qualities of human beings: good people, bad people, criminal people, cruel people, kind people. The analogy came into my mind of the spectrum of colours. You have the violet, indigo, blue, green, yellow, orange, red. Without the spectrum, there is no beauty. On a monsoon day, if you look up at the sky and you see what they call the *Indradhanush,* the rainbow in the sky, how happy it makes people! We need variety to bring unity! Nobody calls red a dirty colour and violet a beautiful colour. And some women prefer one colour over the other, but it doesn't make it dirty or good. They are part of the spectrum. Similarly, I prefer to think that all human beings constitute a spectrum. With one end here, one end there. What is good about this end or what is bad about the other end? A criminal. So what? It is well-known, at least in India, that most of our great saints were sinners. Either they were robbers or dacoits or looting people or womanisers or even worse, murderers. But the moment of change came and there was the saint. Remember what Vivekananda said when talking about women, especially prostitutes! He said, "Look not thou upon my fallen sisters, for if they were not there, you and you and you would be in their position!"

So unless we have this tremendous generosity of love in our heart, not synthetic intellectual ideas of bringing people together, it is like that stupid exercise in bringing together the religions and calling it One World Religion and all that you have is a temple with a shrine for Buddha, one of Christ, one for Allah Miya! That is not a world temple. It is a temple with several shrines. And people of each religion going to each different shrine; there is no unity. In fact, you are emphasising differences there.

So this idea of the spectrum is right, and that without the spectrum there cannot be a white colour—everybody knows! If you remove one of these colours from the spectrum, the resulting blend of the other six colours will not produce white at all! It may be a dirty grey; it may be a dirty something else! Similarly, in our human existence we have this beautiful spectrum—evil, tendentious, contentious, criminally minded people on the one side, the violet end, let us say, and the same wise, the far seers as we see them, the far sighted, the visionaries of the future, on the other end. This is just a spectrum. And anybody who is at this end, if he criticises the other end, he is criticising the spectrum, and therefore himself. The same thing about colours.

The same thing about sound! What is a good sound? What is a bad sound? There cannot be anything that is good or bad in Lord's creation. It **is**! Therefore the Veda says, "Existence, Consciousness, Bliss."

So the idea of diversifying things, differentiating things, of this arrogant idea that I am helping to raise people from one level to the other, it would be as stupid as the red end of the spectrum saying that it is creating intelligence in the violet end of the spectrum and making it red like itself. The only possible way is to let the Creator, the one who created the spectrum, blend it back into one harmonious whole again, and this is the work in which we are involved. We are not, I repeat most emphatically, trying to reform people here. We are trying to make them blend into a unity which is what Sahaj Marg should become. In Sahaj Marg there will still be people of varying intelligence levels, of varying consciousness levels, because these two are the same things, of different abilities or capacities to absorb the teaching. Nevertheless they are parts of one whole and the whole cannot exist without the parts.

The nine o'clock prayer is designed solely, exclusively to make us conscious, that, "I am part of that vast humanity which we call the brotherhood. If they fall, I fall with them. If tomorrow there is trouble in Communist Russia again, the whole world will shake with that problem, not only the Russians. If there is internal revolution and somebody is overthrown there who has been responsible for all these things, again the doors will be closed, tighter! It will take several centuries to open them again.

You all know how difficult it is to open the doors of a temple which has been closed for a hundred years. Sometimes you have to batter it down, break it down; that is what happened to the wall of Berlin. Never allow to be closed what has been opened. Because if you permit it to be closed again, it will be closed tighter and you cannot open it again. Most of all, this applies to the door of your heart. We all know by personal experience, experience with every one of ourselves, with the world, that very often there are moments when even, not out of fear, but out of some inner compulsion, we allow the heart's door to open and there is utter confusion, utter fear; instantly we tighten it up again. Next time, to open it again becomes more difficult. A moment of sympathy for another human being, a moment of unseen help to somebody and we are ashamed. Why are we ashamed of doing good? Why are we ashamed of helping to raise a man who has fallen on the street, that we tuck our umbrellas like the good British back into our armpit and walk on as if we have not seen this happening. Why? Because when we confront this act of kindness, this act of sympathy, this act of love, it is blinding to our senses. "Oh, my God! If I do this again and again, where will I be? I will be lost." So we close the door tightly, put double locks on it, and throw away the key. Seven thousand years later the next Special Personality may be able to help such a person again.

So this nine o'clock prayer is to open your doors. Forget humanity! There is somebody who will take care of humanity. If the good Lord up there had to depend upon our nine o'clock prayers to liberate humanity from its doldrums and bondage and misery and cruelty and ignorance, God help God! It is to help **ourselves**. Everything else we do in Sahaj Marg is –self-centred. I meditate for myself. The prayer is said for myself. The next: cleaning my grossness. The bedtime prayer for my good sleep, dreamless sleep, nightmare-less sleep, so that I may wake up again in the morning. Which abhyasi wants to go to sleep and sleep eternally? One hand, if it is raised, I will give a special sitting! [laughter]

So this is the fraud that we are perpetrating— not on the creator; He is beyond fraud—on ourselves. We want to wake up, wake up better, better qualities, more ability to make money, more ability to cure more patients, more ability to have more clients. This is what we are doing in Sahaj Marg! Cheating ourselves, pretending to be good abhyasis. "Sir, I do my cleaning at night and prayer meditation. But sometimes I am sleepy, so I just do it for seconds." It is like my grandson who gives a sitting. He closes his eyes and it is finished. At least he is able to do that much.

So, I think my Master, in his tremendous generosity, said, "Three things you are doing for yourself: morning meditation is patently for yourself. Cleaning: for yourself by yourself. Night prayer meditation; again by you for you." Why not you like to liberate yourself from this personalisation of this yoga and widen the context of your approach to include everybody else? This, to my mind, is the real meaning of the nine o'clock prayer. It is to liberate us from our own narrow, selfish, self-centred selves, make our heart open, that everything I do, I do for all! Everything I do must be for all. Everything I do must benefit all, otherwise there can be nothing in creation which can only benefit me. Please take this as an absolute spiritual law and truth, that nothing I do can benefit only me. If somebody is vulgar enough to say, "What about your toilet function?" Yes, everything I eat I excrete; it goes into some farmyard; it is a manure for something else, too. Of the ultimate desecration of the human values, when I die and if I am buried, the worms will eat my flesh. Even my death has to benefit somebody. If my death must inevitably benefit others, why not my life benefit others?

So, brothers and sisters, forget all these high-flying ideas of sacrifice and karma yogis and this, that, and the other. There is no karma yoga, there is no sacrifice. If my life cannot benefit all, my life will be extinguished. I have often used the example of a candle in the West. I may like a candle for myself, when it is dark. But I cannot tell the light of the candle, "You shall burn only for me." Inevitably the light will spread. There used be an old system in our olden days when we had no electricity, that in the evening the mother of the house put a lamp in the window, to guide back the children who have not yet come home. A lamp in the window; an oil lamp is enough to guide a son who is three kilometres away, who can still see it. "There is the lamp of my mother."

If anybody should imagine that we are making wealth only for ourselves, we are eating only for ourselves, we are enjoying with our families only for ourselves, disabuse your mind of such fallacies, self centred fallacies, silly fallacies, stupid fallacies!

Everything I do must inevitably have its reverberation throughout the universe, not only this world of mine! Throughout this universe! It is not for nothing that in the Christian Bible it says, "A sparrow cannot fall to the ground without the whole universe vibrating to that fall." That is why our thoughts are so potent. That is why we must learn to regulate our thinking. That is why we have to meditate. Therefore, all meditation eventually must result not only in the mediator himself becoming a model example of a divinely humanised being, but as a lamp for the rest of humanity, for the rest of Eternity. This is the purpose of Sahaj Marg. All the *angas* of Sahaj Marg are finally aimed at this purpose of divinisation of the whole universe. Anyone who says, "This is mine. I am meditating. The benefit of this meditation shall be mine," is betraying this function, this purpose of Sahaj Marg, and therefore a betrayal of the Master. Whether you like it or not, you have to understand this. Whether you do it or not, you have to do it, because if you don't do it, you perish. If you do it, everybody succeeds.

Thank you.

71

Spirituality in Management

Some years ago when I was first asked to speak on a subject like today's, 'Spirituality in Corporate Management', somebody remarked that "It is strange bedfellows, spirituality and corporate management." I was inclined to agree. After Mr. Rajagopalan's introduction, I was reminded of my dual role in life—spiritual life from my corporate life, trying to behave like a manager in my office and like a spiritual person in the ashram.

I started life as a salesman. I didn't have to do much with management, but I had to slowly grow into my role, first as a salesman in the field, then as a salesman controlling other salesman from the office, as a sales manager, then slowly into corporate executive functions, to the extent that I was able to remain a human being and not just as a slave driver. I was able to be more and more successful in my job. I had more and more contented people working for me and, *ipso facto*, my boss was also more happy with me. I think I owe my success to this, starting as a 150 Rupee salesman in a company and ending up as an Executive Director in the same group. Managing several concerns in that group was not easy. Like a jumping frog, jumping from stone to stone, today the opportunities are so vast, you can start on 500 and end up on 5,000 in a couple of years. But in my days it was not so easy, and certainly not in one company. It was a small company when I started, substantially bigger when I

Talk given at Ritz Hotel on 2 February, 1990

left it and, being a privately owned corporate edifice, it had the advantages of personalised management, and to some extent, the advantages of modern business methods, which were not very palatable to my bosses, because they thought they would lose their hold on the companies. Private ownership is always suspicious of modern technology and modern techniques, because what they cannot personally control, they believe is inimical to their interests.

So that was also one of our jobs. My colleagues and myself had to satisfy the partners of my organisation, that like when you telephone somebody, you don't lose contact with him just because you don't see him. You are still able to speak to him. If you have a computer, you are certainly not handing over your management and your finances to other people. You are only handing over some part of the function to them. Enlightened management means management of various things with absolute subtlety, not with a heavy hand, but as if you don't exist. This is my personal knowledge that I have gathered over twenty-five to thirty years of experience. Like they say, "No Government is the best Government." Drawing an analogy from that statement, I have often found that no management is the best management. We tend at the higher levels of management—it was one disease I had to face and overcome—we tend to believe too much in our own importance. It is necessary to believe in ourselves, but not in our importance. This is a distinction which I would like to you to appreciate. Belief in oneself is not belief in one's importance, or belief in one's infallibility, or even belief in one's own necessity to run things. If nature teaches us things, if the shocks that we have experienced in our own Indian existence over the last fifty years indicate anything, it is that no human being is absolutely necessary to any situation—**any** situation. If the country can run without a prime minister, if states could be run without kings, and if the whole thing could be converted into a democracy and if people who have nothing to do with ruling a country could become rulers overnight, it is a system that works, and we have to use a system properly. It is very much like a human being has to learn to use his personal system, his body, his psyche, his soma, his intellectual functions. If you let any one of them run away, you suffer. The beauty of the system is that we have an absolutely impeccable system given to us, where you think of the human being as a corporate edifice, which he is, because the word corporate comes from the word 'corporeal'—corpus— a body.

So what is corporate management about? It is the management of a body, and if you draw the parallel with a human system, it has its own functions: it has its ingestive functions, it has its digestive functions, it has its excretory functions. Raw material going in, finished product coming out, waste products being thrown out, whether as an effluent or unnecessary waste, and we control all these functions: Finance Management, Capital Management, Men and Matters Management - these are all accessories, adventitious functions to the main purpose of existence. It is like a man who eats too much and cannot excrete, or like a man who is not eating enough and excreting all the time, not able to retain.

So if you are able to take a hint from nature's lessons, I think any intelligent man who has learnt to master himself and master his own functions independently and collectively as a totality, as a unity, is a good manager, whether he is in corporate life or not. I mean, we are all in corporate life, for that matter, as long as we are in this body. The day we die we are no longer in corporate existence, either here or in the body. It is my humble suggestion that one who cannot manage himself is useless as a manager, even though he may be a chairman of a big corporation.

I believe personally that what the Hindu religion calls the theory of samskaras, *karma* is often responsible for where we are. It is a distinct facet of my Master's teaching that there are two existences we participate in: the material existence is ruled largely by what we bring into it in the shape of our past destiny which we have created for ourselves. This should explain, if you are able to think about it, why apparent nincompoops occupy top positions and geniuses occupy positions way down in the ladder of corporate life. Of course, we are able to explain a genius occupying low down position, we say, "Poor fellow, his destiny is against him." But when it comes to ourselves, as chairman and managing directors and what have you, it is not so easy to be so humble and say, "I am here because of my past destiny, not because I am a great guy in management."

I think a pinch of humility is always good, not that we preach humility as a necessity, but because it always makes us cautious. If I know that I am where I am by the grace of God, and without it I would be where the other fellow is, and if I can attribute my success to what I have created for myself in the past, the scenario that I have created for my past, for myself in the past, I would always be cautious about creating the future for myself in the present. This is the crux of the spiritual teaching of this great land, with its great, enormously great heritage of spiritual values, that the present is created by the past, the future shall be created in the present. Don't therefore bask in the glory of what you are. Know that there are better things to come, provided you have the guts, you have the ability, you have the humility to understand that you are yet somewhere only in the middle of the ladder, even though it may apparently be the end of the ladder upon which you are now situated.

So the whole focus of a successful life in any field of endeavour, whether as a *kshatriya* in the war field, whether as a Brahmin in the sphere of teaching and advisory capacities, whether as a *vaishya* in agriculture, whether as a *sudra* in service, borrowing the categorisation of our great Vedic texts, is management of the self which is responsible for success in any of these fields, and we have seen this again and again in the lives of the great saints of the past, great warriors of the past, great kings of the past. The great warriors were those who did penance, not who brandished their weapons and went practising archery in the fields.

The great story of Ekalavya is a pointer to this, that when his guru refused him, he could make a *putli* of his guru—statue of his guru— and by worshipful obeisance and an attitude of humility, accepting that stone idol as a Master, he could become the master archer, of whom Drona had to be afraid that he would defeat Arjuna and so he took away his thumb.

So this is what worshipful attitude to your service, to your work, brings about. I am greatly appreciative of our two epics which are being shown on the television, whatever may be their commentaries. Some people say they are too filmy, this, that and the other, but they have brought home to our households truths which we have long forgotten, which we could not afford to forget. The greatest emperor ever in India was supposed to be Raja Janaka not because he was a great emperor of a great territory but because he was a spiritual ruler. He was a *Raja-rishi*, a very rare phenomena—a king who was also a rishi. You will all recall when Dr. Radhakrishnan became the first President of India, they called him the 'Philosopher President', not without substance. Where the two meet, is true greatness. Where there is isolation in one sphere there is something wanting. The whole idea of a spiritual education in which we are trying to participate, is to bring the two halves of existence together into one blended human being, who is balanced in all his functions, who has his spiritual approach to life, whose goals are essentially spiritual, whose corporate life is only an aim or a method to carry him through life. It is very much

77

like we use a boat to cross a river. Of course, great emperors have had boats gilded with gold and silver and things like that. But if the wood in it had failed, they would have sunk.

So the spiritual education is what we call the ability to make your self into what you have to become: a balanced person. In our Sahaj Marg system, the tradition is not to become super human in any field. Not a *dhanurdhara*, you know, *sarvasreshta dhanurdhara*, not *sarvasreshta gadhadhara*, not a political man like Chanakya, but someone in whom all the faculties that nature has blessed us with are balanced, because it is in balance that perfection lies.

So, in management, when you have been able to master this need for balance in your personal life, the outgoing tendency with the in-going tendency, the need for anger with the need for humility, the need for arrogance with the need for pride with the need for humility again, assuming postures which we may have to assume in management functions, but not becoming involved in those things as if you yourself are that.

Remember the famous story attributed to Ramakrishna Paramahansa about a snake which became a Guru's disciple and which he saw after ten years. Children were throwing stones at it and poking it with sticks, and the snake was almost dead. The Guru said, "What has happened to you? You are my *chela*, isn't it?" The snake said, "Lord, you taught me *ahimsa* (non-violence). This is my destiny. Even children mock me today." And the saint said, "Stupid fellow, I didn't ask you to lie down like this and be poked about. Why don't you hiss? You don't have to bite!"

So we have to stage-perform our functions. A manager must pretend to be angry, must pretend to threaten, all these pretensive actions, we have to play. The moment you are angry—any man here who has been negotiating with labour and unions knows this—the moment you are angry, you've lost the battle. You cannot afford to be angry, but of course, at a bargaining table you have to pretend to be annoyed, you have to pretend to be displeased, you have to stage a walk-out, you have to come back, shake hands, sign the agreements! What is that you are really doing? You are managing yourself, and a capable personnel manager is the one who has been able to manage himself, exactly playing the part that he has to play, giving in where he has to give in, holding back where he has to hold back, detached from the scene, as if he is a robot performing precalibrated functions. If he is involved and if he makes the mistake of thinking that he is doing the negotiations and he can walk away from a table with thirteen union leaders or thirty-five union leaders, he will no longer be the manager of personnel next year. Same with finance management. If you think that the money you are handling for your corporation or for your bosses is yours, God help such a management. It is somebody's, it is on trust. Administer it as a trust, take wise decisions, don't be involved in the success or failure of it. You have only a right of decision. You have no right over the ultimate end of that decision. What the karma yoga theory of Bhagavad Gita says very clearly: *Karmanye vaadhikaraste maa phaleshu kadaachana.* Every businessman knows this. Every man who has managed businesses knows this. Notwithstanding the latest fourth generation computers, any business decision can go wrong or, aping the Peter principle, anything that can possibly go wrong will go wrong. It is way of nature. There again, if you have to come to the decision with a prayerful attitude, with a humble attitude, that "I can only do what I can, the rest is with you"; it is not that we beg God to make ours a success; it is that things should be right. Success and failure are personalised equations, personalised values, self-centred. But, is what I am going to do, good as a general thing? Is the product that I am going to launch on the market tomorrow, good as a general thing for human beings to consume or to wear or to go fast, whatever it may be. Few corporations today have the ability to think this way; they don't even wish to think this way. In America you have these consumer protection organisations and the famous scandal about tyres some twenty years ago, when I was still a salesman. It is because corporations are only interested in making more money and more money and more money. They will take everybody else. But the moment you forget that the consumer is a human being, who is your friend and in whose position you may be, either before you joined the Board or after you retire from the Board—we have all seen cinemas where, unfortunately, the *Marwari* is shown always as the villain of the piece, who makes spurious drugs, and his own son succumbs to that drug when he is sick. This is retribution. This is nemesis. All the more reason to think of human values when you work as big bosses in empires, corporate empires. It is very easy to sit at the top floor penthouse, air-conditioned and completely divorce yourself from the rest of humanity. It is an illusion which is easily engendered in corporate life. I say this to you with the conviction of experience, because I was almost trapped.

So we have to retain touch, like a human being where his head may wear a crown, but his feet must be on the earth. He may wear velvet and walk with a golden crown on his head, but his feet will still trod the dust of the roads. We have to keep contact with two elements, **this** and **that**. The human and the product. Are they good for each other? Am I doing right in doing this? Is it good for everybody, including myself? Bearing in mind that what is only good for me and not good for others will eventually break me, because nature does not permit individual goodness. If a saint is a saint only for himself and refuses to cast his light on humanity, he is a fraud, he is a betrayer of the principles of Divinity. And he is destroyed. You cannot have a lamp which illuminates only one person. The light will shed, whether you like it or not, on everybody else in this room. You cannot have rain only on your field. Others may be prepared or not prepared to receive the blessing that rains down from Heaven. That is their fault. But nature provides everything for everybody and it is our business to harness nature's resources and make the results of that harnessing available to everybody. This is, I suppose, the ultimate idea of socialism—not some political idea of socialism that everybody has a right to vote and things like that. He who does this, he who gathers to distribute, he who manufactures to supply, retaining for himself but only what his own meagre needs are, will eventually be the successful man. Not successful in that he has a Cadillac or a penthouse flat and a boat on the Caribbean, but as a successful man in himself, with an idea of success in his own heart, content with himself, at peace with himself. He can sleep peacefully without having to answer any questions from anybody, because his conscience is clear.

As far as management is concerned, if you look at the famous Upanishad where you have the *ratha* with the five horses and the two wheels and the Master of the chariot inside and the driver holding the five pairs of reins, there can be no management education beyond that. I don't know why we have to read Japanese books on management and Harvard books on management and buy series of them at twenty-four thousand rupees a set. I was also enamoured. I have several volumes of those which I never read, to tell you frankly. The pride of possession, not of learning, not of using that knowledge, but just when people came and saw my library, with all the hard-bound books in gilt and red covers, it was a very nice feeling. This Upanishad tells you that there is a chariot with five horses, there are five pairs of reins, the Master is the Soul seated therein, serene, calm, unconnected with anything else, the driver is your *buddhi*, the two wheels are the corporeal and incorporeal life, the road is the road of destiny. How to balance the five horses? How to make them not run away with you? How to keep a light and gentle hand on the reins and yet control the horses and make them perform not only adequately but perfectly? How does the Master give instructions from within? This is the aspect we have lost touch with. All the rest we have followed. We are masters of management. We know how to manage the horses, how to keep the chariot on the road, but we have forgotten the Master behind, who is the owner of that thing, the soul within.

Most of our travails of today, the troubles of today, the tribulations of today, the disease, the misery, the mental agony that we suffer is because we have lost touch with the inner owner of ourself, the Lord of ourself, the Master within, and therefore we are blind. As my Master would put it, "Such a person is at the mercy of his karma, his samskaras." He may rise, he may fall. It is not his success or his failure. It is the success or failure of his samskaras. He who has been able, by the grace of the Master and by a great deal of sustained personal effort, to remove the samskaras altogether, can claim to be a free man who now has his destiny in his hands. He is now able to take decisions as he takes them; his own decisions, not decisions enforced upon us by a latent samskara within.

We are all robots, pretending to be alive and to be cheerful and happy and married and with children. It is a robotic existence. I mean, if any of you would care to examine your own conscience deeply at night when you are not able to sleep, you will find the truth of this statement. When do the samskaras cease to influence us? That is when the past has no longer any hold upon me. I am now literally liberated and I am a free agent in the hands of Divinity. Now I can shape my destiny. Otherwise, even my destiny is a push from behind. It is like the blind forces of evolution. Nobody knows what this stage is going to evolve into. It is at the play, at the mercy of a push from behind, of what they call certain forces which lead to mutations in between. All accidents of nature therefore take billions and billions of years for a stage to evolve into something else.

The human being has been endowed with intelligence and a will power to create his destiny for himself, to become what he must, if possible tomorrow. This is not a corporate career where, to rise from the salesman to the board should take thirty years. I mean, few people do it, in any case.

So, the crux of management, whether at the board room, or at the family home, or even of a holiday, is personal management—not **personnel**, but **personal**. He who is a master of himself is a master of everything else. Such a person can be anything that nature makes him do at its need. He can be a king when he has to be a king. He can be a rishi in the forest, which means he has to be a rishi in the forest. He can be a warrior on the field. The great ones of the past, Parasurama and Janaka, were everything at the same time. They were advisors, they were rishis, they were *tapasvis*, they were kings, they were warriors, name it, they were that. Today we only produce narrow specialists, whether it is in corporate management or in our hospitals, or in any field that you see. Narrow specialisation with no knowledge of accessory functions, adventitious functions, and we have a mutual admiration society which we call our management institutions and management associations where we congratulate each other, pin needles on each other, Rotaries, Lions Clubs. We are indulging in this game of self deception too long. Forgive me for saying this, but this is the disease of today. Whether in India, whether in Europe, whether in America and the higher we rise in the material existence, the greater this self deception that everything is nice with me, because I have a car and a nice wife and beautiful kids in the best schools. You ask a man, "Why are you happy?" He says, "Well, I have every reason to be." A really happy man is one who says, "I don't know," because that is natural.

"Why are you wise?"

If you say, "Because I have a Harvard degree in Business Management," it is a dependant. "Well, because my Master made me so. My God made me so. Nature created me to be wise." If you ask Vedavyasa how he became wise, he wouldn't have been able to answer you. He had no degrees to show. Valmiki had no degrees to show. Ganesha, when he was asked to be the scribe, had no degree. He was not even a human being. Forget the fact that they are supposed to be gods. These *puranic* stories only show us that anything can be made to perform if there is a right Master willing to infuse the right spirit into that instrument. I mean, a pen in the hand of a man with poor handwriting will only produce a poorly written page of a letter. In the hands of a caligraphist it would produce a beautiful calligraphic piece of work. What is a pen? It is only an instrument.

So, as my brother Rajagopalan said, the first necessity is to accept that we need training. Master, God, these are all terms; if God can be a servant, we call him a servant. In many stories He has come as a servant of humanity; He has come as a protector of humanity; He has come as the destroyer of humanity; He has come as the preserver of humanity. We see the three great functions in Brahma, Vishnu and Maheswara. But there is the creative function which is superior to them in the original act of creation, when the original power descended and everything came into existence without any planning, without any thought behind it. These people are only sustaining that creation, like we managers are only managing something somebody created for us. Somebody established a company, we are recruited, we manage it. To the extent that we should identify ourselves with that purpose it is good; to the extent that we identify that purpose as our own, it is tragic, it can be disastrous. I am employed to fulfil the purposes of a corporation. Good! But its purpose, if it becomes my purpose, there is a subtle exchange which can be as disastrous as in the transference between a psychoanalyst and his patient. This is a potent menace to every corporate manager and to which most of us succumb at some time or the other. It is **my** company, it is **my** purpose, and one day we are thrown out by the neck and we go wailing around, "I made that company mine, I did so much for it, I brought it up like my own baby." Who asked you to? See, a warrior fights on the field, but it is not his war. This lesson we must learn from the Mahabharata. Thousands of people put in the front line at the whims and fancies of the two factions. No soldier ever fights his own war. He fights for somebody else. He is a mercenary. Every man is a mercenary who works for somebody else. And every manager, every chairman of any corporation, even the giant corporation like Ford Motors or General Motors is a mercenary because he is still concerned with his stock options, with his holiday options, with his insurance options. He who works for himself is the free man, the liberated man, because he works on himself, for himself, by himself, to make up himself that idealistic thing which we call the *Purusha.*

So, this is a broad idea of spiritual life in corporate management in both the senses that this corpus and this corpus are identical for me. This is the field. This is myself as the player in the field. If you think of the famous chapter of the Bhagavad Gita: *The Kshetra and the Kshetrajna,* each of us, by the destiny of the past that we have created by our thoughts and actions of the past, have created a field for ourselves into which we descend. It is not an accident. In this field, if we play our part correctly, detached from it, with the idea of evolving out of it into something else, we are successful in the spiritual sense, in the real sense. Otherwise, we may be successful warriors on the field, perhaps dead, perhaps with a Victoria Cross, as in the old days.

So ladies and gentleman, sisters and brothers, I have only to say in conclusion that we have created the field in the immense wisdom of the soul between the lives, the past, and the present. It is the only field in which we have to evolve. Whether it be religion, whether it be the way in which you are born, whether it is language, whether it is the custom, society, what have you. In that field we have to learn to evolve out of that. And he who evolves out of that field into successive higher fields and keeps moving, not attached to any field whatsoever, is the really liberated, ultimately personalised, humanised, divinised individual.

Thank you.

Oneness

I really don't know what to say because the experience is his and not mine. It is true that the Basant has been a very special celebration, but I think the speciality of Sahaj Marg is that everything is more special than the previous one. That's all. So we should not say, "This is it!"

I think this is the lesson that we have to take from the *mahaavaakyas* of the Vedas: *Tattvamasi.* That thou art. This can never be it; it is always that which shall be. So by the very nature of our goal's definition, the goal is infinite, therefore we are ever approaching the goal, perhaps faster and faster in more remarkable ways, in more profound ways. But I don't think humanity in the Sahaj Marg system will ever have a right to say, "Now we have reached the destination." It must also be true that each event shall in some way be more unique than the preceding event, without damaging the uniqueness of the previous event. All are unique. That is why, though we say this was a remarkable celebration, we do not forget that the Calcutta celebration was also a very special occasion, and so was the one in Shahjahanpur at the Tandon Farm. They still remain fresh as unique events. In Sahaj Marg it is not a question of one surpassing the other. It is, each one is a unique and a special part in the whole scheme of things. So we should never make the

Talk at Bangalore on 5 February, 1990.

mistake of saying this is better, more unique. Yes, but certainly not better. Better is a quality evaluation. In Sahaj Marg we have no quality evaluation; more profound? Yes!

This mistake we often find people making when talking of Lord Krishna and Lalaji and Babuji. *Autobiography Volume II* of Babuji Maharaj has led to so much discussion, speculation, futile things. Was Lalaji greater than Krishna or was Krishna greater than Lalaji? Here there is no question of greater and lesser. If there is a strain, there is a continuity of the human race, the essential humanness of the race is always the same. One race may have been more visible historically, not because they were more outstanding but perhaps because they murdered more people. Like we have the famous hoards of Ghengis Khan, for instance. Ghengis Khan is noted not for being a good man but for being a successful murderer on a racial level, mass level. So also we remember Napoleon, Hitler, Nelson, all great war lords, not certainly contributing to human evolution or welfare. They are not noted for having been kind or generous or loving. So greatness is actually a fallacy. Greatness in what?

In Sahaj Marg the greatness is in being a perfectly balanced individual. No exaggeration, no suppression. A person of perfect balance, therefore a Master. So there cannot be a greater Master and a greatest Master and a lesser great Master. These are types of ideas, concepts which do a great deal to damage the Mission's interests. Even to distinguish between a Special Personality and an Avatar, I think, is wrong. What is the difference? We cannot know. Many people I have spoken to, I have told them, "What do you know of the Special Personality? What do you know of the avatar?" People living in the times of Lord Rama and Lord Krishna, distinctly, very certainly did not know what was an avatar, though the avatar was in their midst. Krishna proclaimed himself as being an avatar, as being so many things. Those who choose to believe, believe; those who don't choose to believe, don't believe. Before Babuji's appearance, nobody knew what a Special Personality could possibly be; the term didn't exist. He hinted he was a Special Personality—he never said, he never claimed. He gave some hints, for instance that the Special Personality started working on a particular date in *Efficacy of Raj Yoga*, which we calculate and find it is 1945, it coincides with the establishment of the Mission, so it is a very facile assumption that the two are one, that Babuji and that Special Personality are the same. Even when people had visions of him as the Special Personality, Babuji said, "Well! It is your vision. You may believe it if you like." Well, except for the fact that Babuji said there is such a thing as a Special Personality, we wouldn't know what it is. We would probably have called him another avatar.

So we have to remember that when you need a two horsepower motor and if you don't have it, you are as badly off as when you need a hundred horsepower motor and you don't have it. We need the power or whatever is necessary to fulfil our journey to our Goal. If I have to cross a river, perhaps even a bamboo pole is enough, if I can sit astride it and propel myself. Surely, to cross an ocean, it would be impossible like that. And the man who helps me is a Master. It isn't important whether he is the man who rows the boat or the captain of a ship. Both are performing the duties allotted to them, under their environment. So you can say one did work of a different nature than the other. To say that this work is greater than that, I don't think is very correct. If you don't clean out your toilet every day, but you are a good cook, you might still get a lot of sickness, not withstanding your good cookery.

So what is important, what is not important, depends on an overall view of the scheme of things. Everything is important in life. Cleanliness is important, a certain uncleanness is also important. If you wash out your intestines and make them perfectly clean, we wouldn't live. We can't drink distilled water. So, there again is a balance between purity and a certain impurity that the system needs. It may appear as an impurity to a chemist but it's something we need inside.

So all these concepts of good and bad are all questionable, because they are based on the human level of assessment. What should be the divine level? I don't think in the divine eyes there is anything good or bad. It is **we** who make things good or bad, or see things as good or bad. Similarly, in the divine vision, there cannot be such a thing as a Special Personality, I would submit. For Him, what should be a Special Personality? It is another aspect of Himself descending. It is like a mother with five children. Which is the special child? To the mother they are all her children. One can be a failure, another can be a great success, a third may have died in the third year but she still weeps over it. A mother has no special children. A father may have, because fathers with their egoistic attachment to children and their performance and the reflected importance that they derive from their children's performance, may think of one as a better child than the other. Mother never thinks like that, because the mother creates. For her, all her creation is the same.

So, this way, when we go towards divinisation, we should give up or try to go beyond these concepts, which is precisely what the Gita says: "Give up all these dualities." Don't divide things into two halves and say, "This is good, this bad." When we judge, it is analysis. Analysis means cutting up things into pieces. In a whole vision, it can be neither good nor bad. So, there are parts of the globe which are bad for us. The desert for some of us is bad, the mountains for some of us are bad, the oceans for some of us are bad. But there are people who live in the ocean, on the mountains, in the deserts. So what is really good and what is really bad? When we read of the bushmen in the Kalahari, we are fascinated. "How they can exist?", when we would not survive there perhaps twenty-four hours. So what is good? I say the bushman is good because he has mastered his environment and become capable to lead a human existence, having a family, producing children, looking after them on the barest essentials.

Now to draw an analogy from industry. That productive method is efficient which uses the least inputs. So if you look at it that way, it is not the modern technologically oriented Western races which are really efficient. It is the bushman of the Kalahari who is the more efficient. It is the Arab in the desert who is more efficient, living on a handful of dates and perhaps two ounces of water.

So you see, we have come to get rather twisted and perverted and very lopsided ideas of good and bad, of efficient and inefficient. Efficiency in today's terms seems to mean more and more production, though it may not be necessary. So we have to think in spiritual terms, at least those who are progressing in spirituality. Because if you don't give up these terms of higher and lower, and better and worse, and good and bad, and vices and virtues, we are still going to think of human beings as good and bad, and you are never going to establish a universal brotherhood based on universal love. It's not possible. When you see people differently, you are going to love them differently. It is not possible to love, when you don't see them as same. A mother loves all her children precisely because she sees them as hers. This is **my** child. How can it be otherwise? A father couldn't care; for him it is another drop in the ocean.

So when we come into the field of spirituality, start working as abhyasis, preceptors, and we see the essential oneness of all human being—not the unity of humanity, for Heaven's sake, because that is a wrong conception. Unity is different from oneness, to my mind. My English may be bad, I don't know. But when we see the essential oneness of all humanity, how in the essential things we are all one, how we agonise over the same things, how we aspire to the same things, how our problems are the same, then we find that, notwithstanding the external differences of culture, race, tradition, upbringing, we are yet one.

This is the oneness that we are trying to bring about, striving to bring about. And when we achieve that, we achieve the ability to love all without cutting them into bits and saying, "I love her; I love him," like that. "I love humanity." From there we progress, I suppose, to other forms of life, to include other forms of life when we recognise that the life in an animal is the same as the life in us. It too is born, it too survives, it too dies. All the functions that we are participating in, it is also participating in. It does not have to own a factory to be called civilised. Industry does not make a civilisation; on the contrary, everybody knows, especially the Western people, that more and more industrialisation has lead to more and more crudeness of human values, falling in human values, separation of the individual, dehumanisation and depersonalisation of individuals. All these are concomitants of industrialisation.

We have developed very perverse, very superficial tendencies because of these vague concepts, even in the gods. Who is greater, Brahma or Vishnu or Shiva? That is why you find quarrels going on with the Shaivites and the Vaishnavites; Vaishnavites and the Madhvas, what have you! That my tradition is better, my God is better. All most crass ignorance. How can God be great or small? And greater than what? Greater than Himself? Can you say that the Great God as the infinite one is greater than Himself as the Smallest? As it says in the Gita, "I am greater than the greatest, smaller than the smallest." Can you say this God is greater than that God, though this is a manifestation and that is also another manifestation. In this sense poorly pitted, can the father be greater than the child? They are manifestations of the same spirit, seeking expression. Can one painting of a painter be different than another painting of his? It is again an expression. He may see that this is different, that is different, this I have done a little better. But to judge one and pay a million dollars for it, and to judge another as trash and put it in the wastepaper basket, is a crude way of looking at things. It's like saying, one flower on the same bush of a rosebush is different from another rose on the same bush. Both are roses, both are from the same soil, from the same plant, from the same twig.

So the difference is what **we** create; by looking at it as, "This is bigger, this is redder"—all this external analysis and assessment. The saint is supposed to see that they are cut from the same bush, and this rosebush and that rosebush cannot be different because they are all roses; white or black or blue or red, it doesn't matter. A rose is a rose! We have to go from differences to commonness. Diversity to an inner unity, what I would prefer to call a oneness, the essentialness, through which we can achieve a universal love and therefore a universal brotherhood. Not because we love each part of that whole, but because we love the whole. When we love an apple, we don't love this part of the apple more than that part of the apple. The taste may differ from one side to the other. Yet we say, "I love an apple." So we should be able to say, "I love a human, whoever it may be." Later on we must be able to say, "I love life, in whatever form it may appear." And yet later we must be able to say, "I love this," and the **this** must be universe. This progression of our spiritual reformation, if I should call it, not necessarily growth, because the spirit doesn't grow, cannot come without a falling away of our perception of differences. And the most tragic part of it is when we judge those above us, whom we have no right to judge, whom we cannot judge, because until we reach a level there we cannot judge that which was and which is and which has been.

So while I praise brother Hanumanthappa's visions, we should not come to these conclusions of this, that, and the other, X, Y and Z; one, two, and three. One is greater than nought; smaller than two; two is smaller than three; in what way? The fundamentals of mathematics say all figures are added when you add one to itself. This is basic mathematics. One added to itself over and over again produces everything else, and if I can add myself to myself, which is what we are trying to do in spirituality, growing means becoming more and more of yourself. More and more of yourself means you are isolating or transcending your earlier self in your present self, which you shall transcend again into something else. Not become bigger or better— transcendence.

So this is the way of the spirit, transcending things, transcending existence itself, transcending the environment, transcending finally, to reach a level from where no more transcendence is possible; that is the ultimate stage. I hope you'll all have this idea, strongly embedded in your minds, no longer to distinguish West and East, white and black, man and woman, child and grown-up. These are all transient stages in the full manifestations of that which is ever perfect. Such imperfection as we see, is what we see because that imperfection lies in us, therefore when you see something as imperfect, remove the imperfection in yourself and you will see that as perfect.

So I hope this will be the urge within us that shall develop and lead us inexorably on the path to the final stage of our evolution.

Thank you

Life and Death

I have some work to do. This is one problem that each one feels his work to be more important than the other person's work. His work is to complete the session. My work is to complete everything. I have to oblige him. He is my boss here. I jokingly said the other day, when we had a lot of overseas people coming, that there is always the danger because he is the Inspector General of Prisons in the Karnataka state. He might put us all into one wing of his central prison and close the door. That would have been an easy way out. But there is a moral we have in that sort of story. That when we go to the Master's home, often I have felt that he should lock us up there. Because this idea of freedom, that we can go in and come out when we like, often makes us go away, and few remember to come back. It is an astonishing thing, for those of you who are interested in natural sciences, especially nature, the facility with which things go back to their origin. Birds go thousands of miles and come back to their home again, crossing oceans, crossing vast deserts. Fish go out into the oceans and go back again to their original place. They have no time; they have no compass. But we human beings have been blessed with so many faculties: physical, mental, intellectual. But we seem to be only capable of going away from our home all the time.

Talk at Bangalore on 18 February, 1990

So it is not faculties which contribute to our progress towards our original Home; it is not our intelligence, it is not our bodies, it is not our mind. It is something else. That 'something else' is what we have to find and, having found it, to go by that alone now.

Tom's speech about what is destined and what is free should provoke everybody to think and decide once and for all that really we have no choice. The physical life, the material life is, of course, fixed. I would not use the word 'destiny' because it brings an uninvolved God into the picture. Because we have created what we call our destiny, it cannot be changed, because we have done it. It is like a man who puts himself in prison, locks the gate, and throws away the key forever. He cannot get out anymore. So he brings somebody else to come and open the door for him to get out. In that sense the physical or the material life that we have to lead is definitely a fixed life. When we appreciate this, we should appreciate the other point, that the spiritual life is not controlled by our destiny, because we never thought about the spiritual life in the past. Had we given some thought to it, perhaps we would have laid the foundation for a spiritual life, too. Because that, too, is something over which we have control. It is precisely not available to the large bulk of the human race, because they don't give thought to it; they don't do the preparatory work for it. Therefore it goes abegging. Now when the Master enters our lives, I would venture to say that the physical or the material aspect of our existence he leaves untouched for two reasons: it does not need to be touched; secondly we have to undergo the *bhog* of samskaras which are educating us in a moral sense and this education is very relevant and very necessary.

But here comes the distinction that, whereas for us there is no choice, there is no freedom, we feel confined. For him all choices are possible. He can do anything at wish, even interfere in our so-called material destiny if it is necessary. So from the human standpoint and the abhyasi's standpoint the physical life and physical destinies are fixed, because we created it, we planned it, and we have no freedom to change it because we are inside the thing from which we are operating. Like a child cannot push a car from within, even an adult cannot. Even a driver cannot do it. He needs the engine to start. If you just try to push it from within, nothing happens. But He can do what He wishes.

In the spiritual life there is total freedom because it is not something created by samskaras. The spiritual life is not subject to the samskaric laws in the same fashion. There is no action and reaction precisely because there is no giving and taking. There is no having; there is only becoming. And then the law of nature, being one which leads us towards the evolutionary goal, no force on earth or in Heaven can interfere with our spiritual growth once we have embarked on it, unless again we choose to interfere in it ourselves. God, in His infinite mercy and compassion, gives us the freedom to do what we will. He says, "If you want to stop it, stop it, because I am the Master of eternity. For me here, a hundred lives that you waste is but a moment in my time. It doesn't matter to me. But remember how much it means to you." They have their lifetimes of joys and sorrows, miseries, separations, frustrations which can break a man.

Our friend from the bank, the last speaker, was talking of a mere episode involving some scandal, some misdemeanours probably, misinterpretation of rules, giving away facilities that he had no right to give, things of that sort, for which one man even committed suicide. Therefore Babuji used to say, God blesses us with death which is a memory break! Enough! you cannot tolerate any more. It is like the surgeon who operates under anaesthesia, precisely because we cannot bear the degree of pain that we may be subjected to.

So Nature has devised for our protection—you can call them overload protection devices, like you have fuses in your electric circuit which trip when there is an overload to protect the wiring in the house. Similarly, to prevent our nervous and other systems from being shattered by experiences that we are exposed to by our own past which have resulted in the first samskaras, this overload device called death comes. And the biggest mercy is we cannot carry our memories with us into the next life because the overloaded memory is perhaps the greatest problem. Guilt is nothing but memory of a past event interpreted in a much bigger way.

Self praise is another overload accumulation, our own estimation of ourselves, arising out of the memory of the past. A rich man gives some charity daily. And if he keeps account of it he becomes a sinful giver because in his mind he is calculating, one lakh, two lakhs, three lakhs, and one day he boasts, "I have given fifteen lakhs to charity." And that is the overload point for him, perhaps! And when he imagines how much money he has parted with, unwittingly, little by little perhaps, he may have a heart attack and die.

So memory is what builds both self esteem and guilt complexes, and if you carry this from life to life, no human being will have the strength to face himself. So death comes. And when we say who created this death, we build our overload characteristics into ourselves, and this perhaps explains these so-called anomalies, where you find a saintly person suffering, and often ignorant people say, "Sir, how can he be so spiritual and also suffer?" Because his material circumstances cannot be altered. It is his creation, he has to undergo it. "Yes but you said the Master can, if he chooses, interfere?" Yes! But the Master does not choose to. Why does he not choose to? Because he will not be broken by these experiences. They will not interfere with the spiritual life. When will the Master decide to interfere? When he knows this man will break under the load that he is carrying. But is it necessary to do like that? Yes. Why? You cannot have an electrical current wired for zero watts. Then the phase will be tripping every time you put something on and you will be replacing the fuse. "But you, sir, don't you think compassion..." No compassion. The highest compassion is to make him develop to the highest possible extent. And if he can do it carrying the load, that's much better for him.

103

So, the obvious punishments that we are supposed to get over, are not really punishments. They are increasing our load-bearing capacity. And eventually you might arrive at a conductor which can bear infinite loads, which is the Master, the God. For him, no load is too great, no current is too high or voltage or amperage, or what have you. No weight is too much for him to lift; no place is too small for him to get into; no place is too large for him to support.

So if we want to go on the way of divinisation and only think that we shall sit in an easy chair and smoke a hookah, it is a fallacy. After all, Masters suffer more than their abhyasis, precisely because all that the abhyasi cannot support, perhaps he takes, perhaps he destroys, that is his business. So when we talk of destiny and free will, we are really talking of a Westernised concept like mind over matter. There is no question of mind over matter— without mind, matter wouldn't exist. And then whatever we may talk philosophically by saying, "Yes but when you are dead and your mind is dead, won't the world still exist?" Exist for whom, by whom? What doesn't exist for me, doesn't exist. It is a fallacy to think it exists for somebody else. Otherwise you would be happy with the pleasures of other people, even though we are miserable: "Yes, but you know, I am not in pain because they are all enjoying life." But we are not able to say it! We say, "But what about my misery?"

Therefore the universe is very really a highly personalised universe. When I am in it, it exists for me; when I am not, it doesn't exist anymore.

Whether it has an absolute existence is a stupid question to ask, because there is no such thing as absolute existence, accept in the ultimacy of the divinity. Everything else is transient. That one is less transient, one is more transient doesn't make any difference to the principle of existence. That a man lives a hundred years and another lives only three years does not belie death. Death is ever-present. It comes to him later than it comes to me, perhaps, but that doesn't make death something that can come at your choice. You needed that time to come to the threshold of your pain-bearing capacities, your memory-bearing capacities. Now if they are going to hamper your personal development, there is a cut made by the scissors of the omnipotent editor. He says, "Stop. Unwind the reel. Put this back again. It is as if they are two separate existences of this fellow. It is really one, but I in my mercy cannot break him. I have to give him a chance." There is a pause, an interval, during which the soul reviews its past activities, past thoughts, and decides what to do in the next life. It appears as a next life, but it is the same life. It is like a dam where the waters are impounded and the water perhaps thinks, "I have no freedom of movement." But with every foot that it is rising, its energies are increasing. Can you imagine an infinite dam? It cannot exist because infinite water would always break it down.

So this business of death is really a merciful episode in our lives, between two existences on the temporal plane, to give us a pause, to give us time to recoup our energies, forget the past and go ahead with the future. Here, a wise man should do this every day. Every day we go to sleep and we leave that life behind. That is finished. Next morning we should start afresh with prayer, with meditation. It is a renewal. And then the previous day's burdens don't cast a shadow upon the today of my existence. If we are able to do this there is no destiny, the question of freedom does not arise, because one is fixed, the other is unfixed, but can be fixed by Him. As the Master can decide to interfere in my material life and alter the circumstances in such a way as to contribute to my spiritual welfare, I shall alter the circumstances. It can be either way: He can make a pauper out of a king and he can make a king out of a pauper if it is necessary. We are unnecessarily and unfortunately prone to interpret this as circumstances for our betterment—that a man should get promotion in his bank, or his office, or wherever he is, and also in the spiritual world. But if he deserves to be demoted once, just to give him a knock on his head, and force his ego a little, couple of inches tighter round the belt—that is the Master's business.

So please remember, He alters circumstances in ways that are necessary for our spiritual welfare, not to suit our ideas of a good life. The same force, the same entity, the same divinity that we call the Master, can also alter the circumstances of our spiritual life if he thinks this can interfere with that, because essentially Sahaj Marg is a balanced life.

So sometimes we think, "I am doing meditation and I am not progressing." Who are you to progress? He makes you progress. It is like we have got into a train and the engine driver decides to accelerate; we are happy. He slows down and we are miserable. He stops; we are even more miserable. Some stupid people even get out of the train and they miss it because next moment he is blowing his whistle and he is off. So once you are in the train, use it quietly until you reach your destination—this is surrender. So I think, a rather long answer for a very small question.

Now I would like to give a story which has a bearing on what our friend Balachander said about the empty cup. When my son was four or five years old, my brother got from Singapore a doll, about a foot high, a gorilla, a seated gorilla, with a glass in his hand. It was a full glass of wine. This gorilla would drink it and the glass became empty. But when the glass came down again every thing went through the mouth into the arm into the glass again. The wiring was through the arm, which we found out later on. So he was eternally drinking from a cup trying to make it empty. Why I refer to this humorous doll is because if you try to empty yourself by drinking it, beware, it will become full again. You have to throw it out. Most of us are prone to drinking our cups—the last one, one for the road, all these sort of things. "No, no, this is the last one. I will never drink again!" Drink it. It is finished. Back it comes into your glass, somehow! The moral of this is, when you indulge in so-called pleasures and even pain, because there are masochistically inclined people who suffer pain, thinking that it is elevating or liberating, it is wrong. We have definitely to have the bhog of samskaras that are with us. We have no right to seek pleasures beyond that nor even a right to seek pain beyond that. Therefore the old ascetic practices of sleeping on a bed of nails and walking on fire are crazy. They are stupid because you are trying to belie the laws of nature and advance your progress by unwanted suffering. The law does not permit either suffering or enjoyment, because they are two sides of one coin. The law says, "If you do this, this shall also happen." Therefore, perhaps when we indulge in too much asceticism, you find the same man suddenly throwing it all and taking a companion and living nicely, for six years and imagining that it is the fruit of his penance.

So samskaras we have to undergo without even thinking whether it is giving us pain or pleasure. It is like a machine, an engine which runs and becomes hot in the process. It is that the machine tendered to cool it or pour some oil on it or whatever was necessary to be done. It is not aware of its own heat. Even if it is so hot that the wheels seize or the gears seize or whatever it is, it is in the state of benevolent ignorance. Now when we move our perceptive faculties to the field of our existence, we become conscious of these things. The only thing that can prevent this is constant remembrance. Then we don't know what we are suffering, what we are undergoing, what we are enjoying. It is happening to the body. It is going on its way. In that way the cup, even if you drink it does not come back into the glass, because whoever has finished, their samskara is eradicated forever. How can new bhoga or new samskara be created? Precisely by thinking of what is happening. If I am attached to what is happening, creating memories of these things, samskaras are formed and they harden, and then cleaning is necessary. Sometimes you have to take several lives.

It is not so easy to empty the glass. It is very nice to speak of the Divine wine flowing over empty hearts, but we have no empty hearts. Nor can we afford to have an empty heart. Because if it remains empty too long, it may be filled up by something else other than the divine flow. This danger is always there. Therefore we have to instantly substitute the corruption that lies in our hearts, whatever it may be; even the 'good' I call a corruption because that which should not be there has no need to be there and if it is there it is a corruption. Corruption does not necessarily mean evil. To me, corruption means the presence of something that is not necessary to my existence.

So if you are able to do the substituting process, throw this out and bring that in. In such a case perhaps we will have that success of which Babuji says, "Turn your head from here to there and the whole thing is over." So the whole problem is we are always thinking of ourselves. Even when we talk of our progress, we are self-centred. "My progress, my destination, my goal." And if so much of "my, my, my" is coming, where is the room for constant remembrance, where is the room for Master, God?

So one who is really established in constant remembrance cannot even be conscious that he is an abhyasi, cannot be conscious of meditation, cannot be conscious of surrender, cannot be conscious of anything except his beloved. In his

109

consciousness exists only one thing, the Master. And when that stage comes, as Babuji said, "One who can be in constant remembrance need not meditate any more." Because when you meditate, there is the meditation, there is the object of meditation, there is the act of meditation, there are three things, instead of being only one. But it is a step which is necessary to establish His presence in my heart, in such a totality that He is eternally present, and then the whole thing falls off. We now become something like toys which are animated, and when the spring is finished or the battery life is over, it stops. How long it should run, how much power it should be given, in which direction it should move, He determines. We have no more any choice, we have no more any right to judgement. Good, bad, indifferent—anything may happen in the course of this existence. It is according to his destiny that he has fixed for me now. So one of the very great saints of Christianity says, "Judge not that ye be not judged." I would prefer to stop at: "Judge not."

Thank you.

About Miracles

The word 'miracle' smacks a little of unnatural things happening. As if there is a sleight of hand, some hoodwinking, some supernatural powers invoked. I don't deny that Brother Ramakrishnan's brush was cleaned. I prefer to think that he went into a memory lapsed state and cleaned it himself. It has happened to me, too. But it is only a lapse of momentary memory and we are away somewhere and the body is doing things on its own. If I can be asleep and scratch myself and hit the mosquitoes and change my position every twenty minutes without my knowing it, I dare say we cannot call them miracles, though in a sense they are miracles. Because with a minimum of consciousness, my body is able to function. But nevertheless it is wonderful that sleeping in bed I can attack mosquitoes, I can attack ephemeral enemies also in my dreams; so many things happen during sleep.

So in Gita, Lord Krishna says, "*Ascharyavat Pashyati!*" I prefer that because everything is wonderful in this world for one who looks with the eyes of innocence, with the eyes of adoration, with the eyes of acceptance. The sceptic never sees wonderful things because he doubts himself. They go around doubting everything, doubting gurus, doubting prostitutes, doubting prisons, doubting kings, doubting God, doubting everything on Earth. In that attitude if you go around, you seek literally nothing. Although every moment is filled with wonders of creation and destruction. Destruction is wonderful, too. Otherwise children will not break toys. If you study children, even in the so-called cruel children who are pulling flies apart, tearing apart the wings of flies, tearing apart the wings of butterflies, there is a wonder in this mechanism which they are seeking to know by pulling apart things. I had a maternal uncle who would bring the most costly toys of those days; I am talking of 1933 when my grandfather used to bring beautiful toys. In those days all were made in Japan. And the first thing he did was to take a screwdriver and hammer and disassemble the whole thing and we were weeping. When he was twenty-two, I was six. We could not say anything. The power of authority in those days of the joint family was too immense. Yet, later on I understood that in him there was this need to know how things worked. In others there is a need to know how things sustain themselves. How does a flower remain in spite of all the wind that is blowing. Why is it not blown apart? A wind which can threaten to blow me down, yet the trees are not blown down, the flowers are not blown down, the leaves are still intact.

So when we look for miracles, we deny the natural and look for the unnatural. In Sahaj Marg everything is natural. We have no supernatural powers here because the powers that God supposedly wields are as natural as the powers that you and I wield. Nature only gives such powers as we have the ability to use for the betterment of mankind. He gets the highest powers who doesn't think of himself but uses it for others. There is no other law in this matter. No other deservingness, no other qualification. A saint is as big a fool as a sinner and a sinner is as good as a saint except that they differ in the utilisation of power. The selfish man uses everything for himself. The philanthropist uses something for himself and much of it for everybody else. The saint thinks only of others, or should think only of others.

I would like to repeatedly emphasise that in Sahaj Marg there are no miracles. Because I have had people come to me and say, "Can you perform a miracle?" I said, "What miracle?" And I tell them what my Master said, that the transformation of a human being is the greatest miracle that anybody can perform. Any fool can convert copper into gold. Any fool can grow plants. After all, you are not growing anything. You are putting the seed into the ground and watering it. How dare a gardener say, "This is my garden. I am growing these things." If at all they do anything, they interfere with nature, pruning and cutting and throwing off things to produce a giant rose where there would have been a hundred beautiful smaller roses as nature wants. Cutting and pruning is not gardening. To let it grow in its own natural way, reflecting its inner urge to self expression, is nature. And one who can do that is the Master. Therefore in spirituality, especially in the Sahaj Marg system, we don't cut and prune like in other yogas. There are systems where you are sort of decimated and things thrown away and things added. Here there is only a transformation of what is into what has to be.

So when people come to us expecting miracles, naturally they go back disappointed, because there are no miracles in Sahaj Marg. At the same time, for one who has the perspicacity to see with eyes other than these eyes, every moment in Sahaj Marg is a miracle. It is unfortunate that in looking for miracles we forget the wonder that is happening and unfolding before our very eyes every moment of our lives.

Expecting a miracle is a prejudice, a preconception. I have often jokingly told my Western counterparts, our abhyasis of the West, that there was a mistake when Moses brought down only ten commandments. There should have been a eleventh, "Expect not for thou shalt not be disappointed." It is expectation that ruins our lives. In any sphere: expect promotion, you don't get it, you are flat, *chaupat*, as they say in Hindi. Expect your child to pass, and he passes just by the skin of his teeth, again disappointment, though some consolation that he did get through. Why expect? Prepare! I like that old Scout motto: "Be prepared." But we are only expecting all the time. Expecting miracles, expecting to lose suffering, expecting to get additional beneficence, get blessings all the time. Why blessings? I have always considered it a weakness in human beings to go around with hands spread out for blessings. Who shall bless whom? I mean, I consider it a weakness to go into wails and beat my breast in front of even a divinity. If I deserve it I will get it. If I deserve it, God himself cannot deny it to me. If I don't deserve it, God himself cannot give it to me.

So these are very clear messages. We go around poking our noses into philosophy, into archaic systems of education, archaic languages, studying Sanskrit, as somebody said, studying Hebrew, and they all say the same thing, "Prepare yourself. Be deserving, and nothing can be denied to you." When I say nothing can be denied to you, I mean **nothing** can be denied to you. So all this weeping and wailing and breast-beating and the famous wall in Jerusalem, I believe, where people go and beat their breasts and are howling in anguish. What for? If there is a God, he would feel unhappy, he would feel miserable: "Look at my creation. Is this what I created them for? I am here and they are weeping." What for? If you as a father or a mother are at home and your children are weeping, don't you say, "I am here. What are you weeping for? Tell me." "No, no, daddy! We have no trust in you. Can you produce the next meal?" Mother says, "Come to me. It is there in the kitchen." " No, no, but if daddy loses his job, what will happen?"

There are children, especially in the West, I am sad to say, who are fraught with so much insecurity that they don't know if their father and mother will be together tomorrow. Where is the money coming from? Is it coming from the dole, from the government? But they forget there is a God in Heaven, which we repeat *ad nauseum* at every prayer. Him whom we talk about most we deny with every breath of our existence. The Muslim in his mosque, the Hindu in his temple, the Christian in his church, and all morning we are talking of God being great, God being merciful, and with every act, with every breath, with every thought we deny the very things we have proclaimed to high Heavens and we say, "What on earth are we doing?" Is this not the highest hypocrisy? I would rather that I am an atheist, and not talk of God at all, than mouth these empty, measly, phrases again and again without faith in them. Not a single one with faith!

All this because we expect miracles. We don't want to do anything but we want something to happen for us. A miracle seeker, a miracle monger is a useless citizen who expects things to be given to him without deserving them. He prays and wails and beats his breast, "Why not a miracle happen to me, sir? You know, my neighbour started with ten rupees capital, today he owns seventeen houses in Banashankari. Is it not a miracle?"

So when I looked for wonder, I found wonder; when I look for miracles I find nothing. I find the devil sometimes. Because the devil is the real miracle maker. Because he wants to entice people to himself. He shows miracles so that we can be enticed. Therefore my Master always said, "Beware of miracle mongers." If you go for miracle mongers, if you are a miracle monger yourself, you would only find frauds.

This is a definite warning we have to give to our abhyasis and prospective abhyasis. Here we have natural growth, no cutting and pruning, no amputations, not even of the psyche! You are not even asked to throw away your sins or to wash yourself, because Sahaj Marg does not countenance the concept of sin and virtue. "*Sukha dukhe same kritva.*" Yes! You also say, "*Punyam, papam vidurya,*" as the great Veda says. Throw away these concepts of sin and virtue. Who are you to sin and who are you to be virtuous? It is your samskara who does it. Clean it off and what are you? Now you are capable of neither good nor bad. Then Master, what is the purpose of my existence? He shall determine. If now he says, go to the slaughter house and kill calves and cows, do it. After all, did not the Gitacharya ask Arjuna to indulge in a vast slaughter of the Kaurava race? The Hindus, at least the Acharyas, are very silent on certain aspects of our philosophies, at our Vedanta. *Ahimsa*—it is a direct contradiction of the *kartavya* concept of the Vedas and the Upanishads and the Gita. If your *kartavya* is to do it you have to do it. Also the Veda says more than human beings there is nothing. He is the highest yet created. Even the Gods have to come down to this earth. *Na maanushaat shreshtataram kinchit.* And we are wailing, "Oh! I am only a human being, sir." We are seeking to justify every sin by saying, "I am only a human being." But we don't stand up, the giants that we have been created as. We don't reflect the immensity of purpose that God has put into us. We are only wailing for our sins, very much like a gorilla with his hands out, beating his breast and saying, "Look at me."

So when are we going to change? Always wailing, always cheating, always corrupting, always acquisitive. For what purpose? Tomorrow, when I am dead, even my body I cannot take with me. Isn't it? Is there anybody here who is going to take his body with him? There are traditions of some saints who disappeared. I think they are all lies. Excuse

117

me for saying it. I don't believe there is room for such things in Nature. If Lord Krishna had to have an arrow shot into his big toe of the right foot and to die, I don't see how a mere saint of our age can pass off with his body. You must remember the great story of Vishwamitra and Trishanku, whom he wanted to send to Heaven in his body and could not do it. One of the greatest sages, who created the Gayatri Mantra, who made Gayatri come before him, he was denied that. It is not possible, it is not natural. If he could not do it, I don't think anybody else could do it. But we go to such places, worship there, borrow our money there, borrow our hearts there, miserable bleeding hearts, seeking another miracle. You don't want effort. You don't want to give time to these things. But we want a miraculous fellow who will come and say, *"Om krim glym swaha"* (magic mantra) and I am instantly a saint. What audacious nonsense such people perpetrate on a gullible humanity!

I was told of a saint somewhere in the hills in North India. One of our people went to see him. There was a big queue from the morning. Hundreds and thousands of people. Somehow, our man managed to bribe somebody and he was taken in front—bribery works even in temples. And there a saint with all his *viboothi* and *jata*, very saintly as we Indians understand it: yellow clothes, white hair, lot of ash on you, *rudraksha mala*, cunning looks on your face, and you are a saint! He went and he said, "Young man, *beta*,"—you are not a saint unless you call everybody *beta*! —*"Beta kya chahate ho?"* He said, "My Master, I want liberation." He put his thumb on his forehead and said *"Bhum!"* This boy waited. He said, "What are you waiting for? It's all over!" He said, *"Mukti? Beshak."* "No doubt I have given it to you." Now that fellow, of course, didn't believe it. The funny thing is, we go for a miracle and we don't yet believe it when somebody says it is a miracle. Isn't it? I am happy, you see, because this is the natural scepticism of the real seeker inside: this foolish fellow says, "Yes, it is right," this wise fellow says "Beware! *Mukti* is not so easy. *Mukti* can be obtained only by devotion, by love, not by practices."

We practise certain things to create love of the Master, of God, what have you. If in that this fails, the system is useless; or perchance I can say the man who tried this is a failure. Because it is a sacred truth again from the Gita: "Who is dearest to you?" Arjuna asked Krishna. He said, *"Bhakta ati priya"*: To me my devotees are the most beloved. Not the practitioner of yoga, not the *jnani*, not the *tattva*, not the *tapasvi*, but my devotee—*"Bhaktaste me priya,"* you see. I mean, the messages are so clear. We don't want to read, we don't want to understand, we go to stupid fellows walking about in yellow robes, prostrate before them, take what they say as truth, and we are cheated. And unfortunately, when a man like my Master comes and stands before us and talks, you say, "How can he be a saint? He is too simple." No Sanskrit, no mantras, no fees, not even for the purpose of self purification, some *praayaschitta*, the usual eleven lakhs, eleven thousand, eleven hundred, eleven rupees. Something they must take, no? This was epitomised by an American boy who, in Cleveland, way back in 1972, after I had given a lecture to an audience—my Master never used to speak—and when we finished we went out on the pavement. A big strapping fellow came and tapped my Master on the shoulder and said, "Hey, Ram Chandra! How can you give liberation for nothing?"

This concept that we have to pay for everything that we get is the curse of the modern age. Much is spoken about Greek commerce and the middle Mediterranean where it all began— transactions. Today we have come to this fixity of understanding that we have to pay for everything— even to pay for love. It is called the oldest profession, so you must have started paying very long ago, paying for love, I mean, in the market-place. Now if somebody has to pay for love, that man should not be anything other than vastly ignorant; it is one commodity which you cannot buy. If that is true, God cannot also seek to buy it from us, by giving us blessings and tempting us with wealth and power and this and that. The rule that binds me to this creation binds Him to that creation; if I cannot buy love, no less can He not buy love. Then what are we praying and throwing our money into temples and coffers for? Can we buy His love?

So Sahaj Marg is very simple: Go to Him with an open heart. There is no other way. If you close yourself up He cannot enter. So the way of Sahaj Marg abhyas is to persuade you to sit in meditation, revive your memory of that which you have been, the glory of the past, the glory of the original home— I don't mean the glory of the Vedic past or the

Upanishadic past, but the original Home from which we have all come. Its memory slowly seeps into our existence, more and more nostalgia develops; one day we cannot tolerate being here, we have to get back there. That day will come, and we start meditation, this, that, and the other. Slowly we become capable of loving, as Hanumanthappa so frankly exposed himself today. It is the destiny of all of us, because we have expected so much and we are failed in our expectation so much, that we have become sceptical of everything on earth. My heart has stopped responding to you: not to charity, not to mercy, not even to the suffering of others. Today we have become, shall we say, stone-hearted, that we can see a man being killed on the street and just turn your head and walk away. Because you don't want to be involved with the police, you don't want to go to the court to give evidence—who wants to go to court? But when I am involved in an accident and I am attacked, nobody comes to my help, I criticise society: "What is this society, sir? I was being beaten on the street by four hoodlums and nobody came to my rescue?" Yes but did you go to somebody else's rescue? Today, even police don't interfere, I am sorry to say! They say, "What is the use? One MP will call me and tell me to do this, another MP will call and say do that." So they just turn round and walk away. You call them, they say, "This is not my jurisdiction." I mean, a policeman, who is bound by jurisdictional considerations and not by humanitarian considerations, is a shame to his uniform. I have had this happen to me, I have had this happen to so many of my friends, that they go from pillar to post, D1 to D2 to D3 police station, only to be told, "Sir, this is not my jurisdiction, you have to go to Teynampet Police Station." You go there and they say, "What is it, a crime? No, no, you go to crime branch." "When did this happen?" "Last night." "Why didn't you report it immediately? Now it is too late." You see, this is the attitude of the protectors of society. The doctors are fleecing us left and right, the lawyers, I mean, they are at the top of the money fleecing business! It is no wonder that we have lost faith in every thing—faith in Government, faith in police, faith in the legal systems, faith in the medical systems, faith in human beings ultimately.

You will see the tendency increasingly reflected in people going in for more and more of pets. They can trust at least their pets: keeping dogs, keeping cats—in the West it is a big substitution that is going on. Animals replacing human beings in our affections, in our homes. If some of the stories are true, even some people have kept millions for cats. What is the world coming to? Because we have been so much expecting things without doing things to achieve things; we are just idle, sitting waiting for some God to come down and bless us, that we have become hypocritical with society, with ourselves, sceptical of everything, sceptical even of ourselves. I cannot anymore trust myself.

So Sahaj Marg is a very serious, very purposeful venture to create from this denuded, disillusioned, miserable human being something of that original glorious creation of God. It is not something personal. It starts with being personal. You as an individual have to evolve before you can help others to evolve. But you are not the target of Sahaj Marg. Excuse my saying this; don't feel upset or hurt. The target of Sahaj Marg is humanity itself. Much is spoken about the Buddha when he said, "I shall not go to the other world till I have rescued every single human being on Earth." Much is said of this, but when my Master says, "I am here for the human beings and humanity," nobody is understanding that he is saying the same thing. Here also we want words phrased in certain ways which will appeal to us, like politicians who speak before the microphone, "Brothers and sisters," and the whole mass of hundred thousand people go crazy. "Brothers and sisters." He has said it. Vivekananda did the same thing in Chicago. "Sisters and brothers of America." Nobody is listening to that. Why? Because the politician promises you tangible benefits. You shall have a gutter outside your door. I will put a post office next to No. 17A in the neighbourhood. You shall have a temple here. The roads shall be illuminated. But when we offer intangible but very real spiritual growth, he says "But how to know, sir! What is the hurry? I have my family to look after. I am now going to get a loan for my daughter's marriage. Let me finish this. Then I shall come to you." One daughter's marriage is over, you say, "*Emmaiah*, Hanumanthappa, *enaithu?*" He says, "Sir, second marriage now. I have liquidated half the loans of the first daughter's marriage. Now I am going around. Sir, if you can help me. Little prayers to your Master. You say, He is all merciful, all compassionate *salpa daya madi.*" By the time he is able to come to you he is fit only to go to the last resting place.

My Master used to say that the young people who come to Sahaj Marg are blessed, because they come when their minds are sound, when their bodies are sound, when they can do something for themselves. The old come to us out of despair, in desperation. If everything else is lost they come. It is like terminal patients being taken to hospitals. No possibility open. Even the hospital says, "What can I do sir? It is too late! Why didn't you bring him a week earlier, a month earlier?" We have this fear of hospitals, especially in South India. We have a belief that one who goes to a hospital never returns. And we make it happen because we delay going to the hospital until it is too late for anybody to help! Let not this fallacy overcome the spiritual also. Let us not wait till the last moment. You know, our Vedantas and our shastras are telling us lies when they say, "If with your last breath you say Hari or Krishna, He will come to you." Perhaps, but even for Him it will be too late.

Of course, for the older people, my Master always had compassion. I remember, in 1968 or 1969 he took my father to some of the highest stages in spirituality. I was rude enough to go to my Master and say, "But Babuji, I don't think my father deserves it." He said, "Yes, you are right. He doesn't deserve it, but I give him out of my mercy—*reham ka kaam hai.*" And he added in Hindi, "*Boodhon per hum raham karte hain, lekin tum launde jo hai, kaam ker ke lena padega*"—"Young fellows like you will have to work for it and get it; on the old people I have compassion." So when young people seek compassion, it is wrong. When *bhaktas* seek miracles, it is absolutely denying the divine spirit when the divinity itself says, "There is a natural way of growth. Don't look for miracles; there are no miracles." And if somebody here wants to say, "What about the *vishvaroop darshana* that Lord Krishna showed to Arjuna?", it is not a miracle by any means. He was only showing himself as He is in reality. People who say it was a miracle, they are fools with all their Sanskrit knowledge. He revealed Himself in His real form; He had encapsulated Himself into a miserable human body for our purpose. You cannot have a dog preaching to you from here; you will not accept it, or a buffalo, you see. Buffalo may spew the Vedas for a few moments. That shows the Guru's greatness, not the buffalo's greatness. True growth is when the Guru can make you like himself—inside and outside. By giving something, you are only palliating a trouble. You give a beggar something. A king gives you his pearl necklace. What is the use? We are still beggars! So my Master said, "Don't seek anything from Him. Go to Him for Himself." What should we ask of God? Ask for Him. Somebody related the story of Arjuna and Duryodhana going to Lord Krishna, a very valid, very relevant story. Seek Him and find Him and receive Him with your heart, then you have everything because with Him, nothing is absent, without Him, having all we have nothing.

Thank you.

A Tour of Sahaj Marg

I will speak just for a few minutes to give some fundamental idea of what this is all about. People are always asking why we have to meditate, what is the use of meditation? Is not our work more important? Some people even quote the Gita and ask, "What about karma yoga?" Then there is this question, "Why do we need a guru?" Often people ask, "Why do we need a guru?" So I would like to trace the fundamental distinction from the time we are born.

There are two aspects to existence. As we are born and we start to live this life being separated from the mother, we have to go through a process of proper physical life and mental education, the two limbs to our existence, the physical, mental and intellectual existence. Education is supposed to be designed to make us into something, make us educated. *Per se* it has nothing to do with making us wealthy or rich or powerful. It is for *gyana.* Education should make a person educated. Thereafter comes the idea that an educated person must do something to get something. Therefore we look for a job, because we have to exist. We have to eat, we have to sleep, we must have shelter.

So I believe there comes this duality of living, to become something and to do something to get something. But in both cases we have to do something. Education is as much karma yoga as anything else. Fundamentally, I think in India we have lost sight of this fact that we can do something for two reasons: either to get something or to become something. Therefore today we find education oriented only towards employment and money making, and the real values of education are thrown overboard. They don't exist anymore. We have a great deal of corruption in education. Educational institutions, educational fields, rigged up question papers, markers, examiners bribed to give you more marks, influences used even in IAS examinations, admission into the lowest level of schools where you need some money now to give donations, medical colleges, engineering colleges asking for lakhs of rupees, all oriented towards a materialistic life, that I invest now in bribes and donations so that I can make millions later on. Yoga says, "You do something to become something, not to get something. In Uttar Pradesh, Bihar, in these *ilakas,* people ask, "What do we get on doing this?" (*Yeh karne se hame kya milega. Isme kya phayda hain? Munafa kya ho saktha hai?*) These are the terms used by commercial people: *sauda, lena-dena.* They are not fit to be used in an institution where they are taught to become something higher and higher and ultimately to reach the goal of that becoming process, by being something at the end.

So this fundamental difference kindly bear in mind, because there is a great deal of confusion. "What will I become if I meditate?" is a good question, a right question. What will I get? Perhaps nothing. Unfortunately, our *Puranas* and the great stories in the *Ramayana* and the *Mahabharata* where even people meditate and do *tapasya* to get an *astra* or a *shastra* or a benefit, have added some fuel to this fire that we meditate only to get something. *Brahmaastra lao, Vajraastra lao, is astra lao*—we have seen all this every Sunday. You are also seeing that when you have God with you, all these astras are of no use. With one pressure of his big toe, Lord Krishna could depress the ratha and Karna's whatever astra it was, went over. It had no value. Even Brahmaastra will fail. Those who have read the *Ramayana* know that when Lava and Kusha attacked their father without knowing that he is an Avatar *Purush*, Lord Ramachandra of Ayodhya, nothing would work against him. He is the creator.

So my Master, my Guruji, Param Sant we call him, Sat Guru, Samarth Guru, Shri Ram Chandraji Maharaj of Shahjahanpur, he always liked to emphasise that we involve ourselves in yogic sadhana to become what we have to become. In Hindi they call it *lakshya* of sadhana; not to get something. That is why people come often mistakenly to meditation and when they don't get a promotion in their jobs or when their sickness is not cured or when their daughter does not get married in time, they leave. They give up yoga. What we would say, *galat phehami*. We don't come to yoga for getting these material benefits. It is not that yoga denies material benefits. But they are ancillary. If you get it, well and good. Now, I represent a tradition called Sahaj Marg, which is a modified form of raja yoga which my Adiguru, Samartha Guru Mahatma Shri Ram Chandraji Maharaj of

Fatehgarh, whom we take to be the Adiguru of this sanstha, rediscovered this system of yogic transmission which we call pranahuti, of which you find reference in the *Kenopanishad*. It is said that this was available seventy-two generations or something before Raja Dasharath of the *Surya Vansh*. Then it was lost, like so many traditions have been lost. Again the transmission of the Guru's yogic essence into the heart of the *sadhaka*, the abhyasi is meant to make him become progressively like the guru, the guru being in Brahma laya with his creator. As my Master put it beautifully, if A=B and B=C, A=C. So by becoming, by making it possible to achieve this *Brahmalaya* with the *Malik*, the Master, we achieve *Brahmalaya* itself. There is no getting.

Sahaj Marg *paddhati*, which I represent here, teaches that the effects of our past lives or even the past in this life, yesterday, day before yesterday, last year, remain embedded in us in the form of what we call samskaras. According to a man's samskara he becomes, he behaves. In a sense, therefore, no human being is free when he is still carrying the burden of his samskaras around with him. It is like a machine which is wound up and pointed in a particular direction; it goes in that direction. That is why many of you may have noticed that you want to change, you want to give up certain bad habits, you want to develop some good habits with the best will in the world, best intention in the world, but we are powerless, because it is the samskara which is acting.

That is the second tradition in the Sahaj Marg system, of cleaning away the past samskaras by the Guru's grace. When that happens, progressively deeper and deeper, and we are in a sense free of samskaras, then comes the real freedom to do what we have to do, what must be done. Not *manmani*, not what I would like to do, but what has to be done. So cleaning of the individual selves, removal of the samskaras, transmission by the Master of His grace, his essence into us, these two *angas* of our paddhati make it possible for very speedy spiritual development up to the highest possible thing. "Here and now," as my Master used to say. In this life itself, bearing in mind that nothing is known about what is in the future. Any man who wants to create his future must create it now. Even in the Fertilizer Corporation, if you want to plan five years hence, you are doing the planning today, and the execution starts from now. Planning is only bringing into the present the objectives of the future. Here we plan in a very tangible, methodical, assisted way, where the Master is our guide, is our Guru, our philosopher, our friend, our everything. What the Upanishads and the Vedas say: He is our *sakhaa*. He is our all. These major differences, we have failed to appreciate. By and large, we have lost the ability to even understand what yoga is about. Yoga means union with the highest. To become in *laya* with that which we are, originally from which we have come. We have lost the way. We have to go back. It is a process of returning home to the Creator and become merged with Him into one entity, losing the individual identity. As my Master used to say, it is an individual *pralaya*, dissolution of the self, so that it can merge with the higher which is the highest, the Almighty.

So please remember this vital distinction between doing something to get something, and doing something to **become** something. Yoga promises that if you involve yourself in yoga, both are possible, but with this limitation, that our *bhautik* life, our material life is always conditioned by our samskara. No man can claim that a yogi can be rich and powerful. They may have powers beyond our imagination, but they are not the powers of this world. He has wealth beyond the wealth of kings, but they are not the material wealth in gold and silver and diamonds and *mahals* [palaces]. His wealth is of a different nature. His powers are of a different nature. Even to ask for powers in spirituality is a sin, according to my paddhati's Masters, Lalaji Saheb, and Babuji Maharaj. What are powers for? Powers are there to be utilised to do something. Therefore we have no truck with the Kundalini and things like that. Because the Kundalini *shakti* is an enormously powerful shakti. It can shatter the Universe, if it is rightly used. But then it is given to one whose work is to shatter the Universe at the time of *Mahapralaya*, not today.

My Master used to say, all the atom bombs and nuclear bombs of today's enormous arsenal of this world can be destroyed in a second by a yogi of calibre, by just his thought power, sitting in meditation. So while it is wrong to think that a yogi has no powers, it is also wrong to think that we do yoga for powers. If we are yogis in the right sense, yoga abhyasis in the right sense going about the

131

path, going about the necessity of becoming what we should become, everything that is appurtenant to the process of becoming is ours. Therefore in the Christian tradition we have this famous statement, "All this and Heaven, too." One who has Heaven has everything, naturally.

You have the story of the Krishna episode where Duryodhana and Arjuna go to him because the *mahabarata*, the *mahayudha* has started and he said, "One will have me and one will have my *sainiks* and everything else. Which do you want?" Arjuna has the first choice. He says, "I want you." Duryodhana is very happy, at least as is shown in the television. He thinks he has made a great victory and that Arjuna is a damn fool. But then we know the result of that. He who has the Lord cannot lack in anything. But He who has everything else in the world but not the Lord will lose everything he has inevitably one day. So this is the *tattva* of the yogic path. And here we have this very special method where the Guru is able to remove our samskaras by the process of cleaning where, by his transmission, because of his love for us, mercy for us, compassion for us, he is able to pour himself into our hearts in the form of pranahuti, the speediest possible evolution is possible.

So I am just giving you a short survey of what Sahaj Marg is about, what it offers, what it does not offer, so there should be no misunderstanding later and saying, "I came to you for this and this and it has not happened." What is the use of such tall talk about yoga? There are no material benefits. No Guru can ever promise material benefits. If a guru promises, shun him. Material benefits are not conferrable. I once asked my Master, "What is this business of *tapasya* and Indra comes and Brahmadev comes and Shiva comes and grants you a boon." He said, "Gods are mindless beings." It is like one of these dispensers. You put in two rupees and get out a platform ticket. They are not working for your benefit. They are controllers of the Universe. Therefore a guru is necessary. The Divine shakti comes as a Guru with mind, heart, able to judge what you need, not what you want.

Sahaj Marg distinguishes very very carefully between the needs and the wants of a person. Needs you have a legitimate right to expect that they are fulfilled. Want is something you create yourself and then if you want it, it is your business to create it for yourself. If you fail in the process it is your foolishness. If you succeed, perhaps it is God's grace. Remembering these very small but very vital distinctions, I now request our brothers, Bro. A. P. Durai, who is in the IPS and is the Executive Director of Vigilance of Indian Oil Corporation, brother Rajagopalan, who is one of the senior officers of Calico in Ahmedabad, and Mr. Mimani, an industrialist from Calcutta, are all preceptors of this Mission. Two of them will speak in English; Mr. Mimani will speak in Hindi. They will elaborate further on this system. I request your patient hearing.

Thank you.

Why Meditation?

Dr. Chandrika Prasad has, like all people who introduce, made me live up to an image which is not really mine. I had a very humble education followed by a career in a company which made me not so humble. A company career, executive career, I think, often breeds more arrogance and pride than institutions like yours. Of course, there is intellectual arrogance, there is the company arrogance, there is the businessman's money arrogance, so many types of arrogance.

Spirituality means getting rid of all these things. My Master said in a very simple sentence when I first went to him, "You have to unbecome all that you are, before you can become something else." It's like emptying a vessel before you can put something else into it. If you have a vessel full of kerosene oil, you have to empty it, wash it out, then put milk in it, otherwise the milk is gone. So this process of cleaning and emptying and filling is the fundamental yogic process, whatever they may call it in Sanskrit and in other esoteric, arcane languages, but we are addressing intelligentsia—the IIT is supposed to contain the cream of the intelligentsia of the country!

I am always faced by one question: Why meditation? What for meditation? So, I would like to start there. Let us leave liberation and God

Talk at IIT Kanpur on 19 March, 1990

realisation, if possible to the very end. I would like to start off by telling you some stories about my own development. When I was in school, we were exposed to subjects like chemistry and practical laboratory work in a British school which we did not have in Indian schools in those days. I know what I studied in my school in Jabalpur, in Christ Church Boys School upto the Senior Cambridge level, did not exist in the intermediate classes of those days. So we had the good fortune to have a higher standard of education, exposure to what you can term foreign ideas, foreign methods of education.

We were told many stories. One of them was the story of Archimedes, in his bathtub, floating there, and this problem working on him: how much base metal has been added to gold in the creation of the crown, things like that. And of course, I was also in many bathtubs but I never made any stunning discoveries in science, or in anything, for that matter. I used to wonder how this guy, just by floating about in a tub of water, came to this, what you call a breathtaking discovery of science, of a fundamental principle, the Archimedes principle. Second one: the discovery of radium by Madam Curie; again an accident; a photographic plate, with a key on top and that lump of stone on top. When she came next morning the photographic plate had been exposed. Most of us would have said, "Well, you know, the plate must have been bad!" But she went on to discover radium and became famous, got the Nobel Prize, what have you!

So, many of these scientific discoveries are not discoveries in the sense that people looked for them and found them. Even in astronomy, most of the great discoveries were hit and run affairs. Nobody said, "I want to find Pluto," and then found Pluto, or, "I will fix Saturn's rings," and then found Saturn's rings. They were looking for something, they found something else. The genius lay in bringing together what they were looking for, with what they had found, either dissociating it with what they were looking for or coming to the conclusion that this is something new.

I remember also reading about one single planet which was discovered purely as a student's dedication to his own mathematical calculation; when they found an error and he refused to accept that his calculations were wrong and he calculated backwards and said, if there is such and such a body of such and such a dimension of such and such gravitational potential at such a position, this could be accounted for and they pointed the telescope there and they found a planet there. So, accident followed by a lot of thought is the basis of science. Unfortunately most people think that science is some sort of a mystic thing, but if you have the humility to look back into the past and the great discoveries and if you understand what mistakes, for instance, Kepler made in his model of the universe, his concentric patterns, and this and that, and then you retrace the significant steps, as one Nobel Prize winner put it, I don't remember who, every thirty years science has turned upside down. What were proven theories become unproven theories. New theories come into their place. You all know, I expect, that Newtonian physics has been given the by run when Einstein came, and what will happen in the future, we don't know.

So one thing about science is that there is no fixity. The very same thing we say about spiritual life. Human life cannot be fixed. It must ever move. Now the point I am trying to make is, what was it that led Archimedes, for instance, to discover the principle which bears his name? I suspect, after I came to my Master and I developed a certain intuitive ability, I think that the bathtub helped him to relax. When you are floating in water there is a certain buoyancy of the body and therefore, a buoyancy of the spirit, and he had this problem in his mind, he had to discover the solution: how much base metal is in this gold and when he was relaxed and in his buoyant condition, his mind came to the solution because he was constantly thinking about it. The circumstances are purely incidental, fortuitous. Any other circumstances could have made it possible, otherwise every one of us who has been in a bathtub should have won the Nobel prize at sometime in his career. What made Madam Curie discover radium? Same thing! Instead of just writing it off as a bad accident or some foolish fellow's mistake in exposing the film, she said, "Under no circumstances could light have penetrated into this drawer in which I had locked the stuff. Let me examine the stone." Perhaps!

So, it is not science that discovers. It is the human attitude to what you are faced with that makes discoveries, whether in science, in spirituality, or in any other realm. What I am trying to suggest is, if you have that same attitude to an internal universe, which we say is far vaster than the external universe, however vast that may be, twenty million years they say, or twenty million light years! The attitude, that what buoyancy of spirit you get, what relaxation you get in a bathtub, the attitude of integrated, one-pointed oriented thought that arises in such a situation which leads to a solution which other people could not find, shows that a certain degree of relaxation followed by a consistent, oriented thought about one thing and one thing only is what achieves success.

We say in spirituality the same thing, Sit comfortably, close your eyes, try to feel at ease and think about one thing all the time. Thinking about one thing continuously is the definition of meditation. Meditation is thinking constantly and continuously about the same thing. So *ipso-facto* we are meditating all the time. People don't understand this but if you think of the same thing again and again and again, more and more revelation comes to you of what you are thinking about. So, just because the great philosophies are in Sanskrit and Hebrew and other languages like that, which are not easily accessible to us, which we cannot study, we think these are something bizarre, perhaps in an extreme attitude, or something not for us. And of course this idea that the vast universe in front of us is worth conquering or overcoming or penetrating, as we say nowadays, thinking that the human body is insignificant. This is all, I am thirty-two inches or thirty-eight inches or forty-four inches round the chest, and the heart is this much of muscle, no more, and we jump to this rather unnecessary, unwise conclusion that the heart contains only blood, is merely a muscle pumping away to keep me healthy and happy and alive. This is at the bottom of the scientific prejudice against mysticism, spirituality, religion, what have you.

I call it prejudice not out of a sense of criticism but as a original meaning of prejudice, meaning prejudging something without having all the facts at our command—*pre-judice*. And I dare say that if any of you wish to experiment on this, it is very simple. Now research in a laboratory, or in arcane mystic things like astronomy, you need years and years to prove something. Especially in astronomy, in which I dabble even now a bit, I have a so-called stellar interest. If you want to photograph a distant body, you need a huge telescope, you need patience, and you need exposure day after day after day to trace a minute path of motion of that body, whatever it may be—celestial body. Sometimes we succeed, sometimes we fail. Sometimes even the emulsion is spoiled by a few specks of dust, which look like a trace of a celestial body, but it's only a trace of dust. So it is heartbreaking. Whereas, if you go inwards, it is heart-making.

Not every scientific approach has been successful. For every scientific success there have been umpteen scientific failures which, fortunately or unfortunately, are not written about. Otherwise they would fill the libraries of this world and more. So what we suggest in spirituality is the technique, the attitude is always the same. One is oriented outwards, towards the external universe.

Magnificent? Of course, there is no doubt about it. Marvellous? Yes, beautiful beyond compare, undoubtedly! But it would be foolish to deny that, when you turn your eyes inwards, there is an equally beautiful, equally marvellous, equally unimaginably beautiful universe lying here. Spirituality does not say, don't study science; it does not say don't study arts, for that matter. It only says, study that and study this, too. Because, like you use the microscope, you use the telescope. One to look into, one to look out of. So what is the difference if you can look through a couple of optical pieces into biological specimens, and geological specimens, shaved, cleaned and made light penetrable and look there and draw sketches of what you see there: amoebas and whatnot. Why not look inside and see the same thing? The brand of spirituality with which we are concerned is the Sahaj Marg tradition of which my Master Shri Ram Chandraji Maharaj is the great proponent and his Guruji Shri Ram Chandraji of Fatehgarh, was the Adiguru, the founder of this thing.

It clearly states that life has two *angas* or wings, the material and the spiritual. One who is successful, he may be successful, but he is rarely happy, he is rarely balanced, he is generally always frustrated. In fact, today in modern life you find that the more successful you are, the more frustrated you are. I don't think anybody here would deny that. It starts from our student days right in the KG class. I have always felt that the boy who comes first in the first primary KG is doomed to frustration all his life because there is a standard by which he has to live all his life. Once you come first in class, you had it in the neck. Your parents are after you, your relations are after you, your society is after you. If you come second next year, they say, "What is this? You have come second." Whereas a boy who came tenth can come fifteenth, nobody bothers about it. Success is very dearly paid for, with peace of mind, with unnecessary effort.

Today, you see, I don't know what it is here, but in Madras, people who get 100% marks still don't get admission in the IIT, which is supposed to be some sort of a dream of education. 100% mind you, the second boy gets 99.8%, third gets 99.8% but he is ranked third because of some quirk of the professors who mark it. Fourth 99.6%, between 99 and 100 there are eighteen rankers and then you have considerations of forward, backward, reserved, this, that, and the other. Frustrations...and a boy who gets 100% doesn't get admission into the IIT and then he has to go for some Economics or I don't know what! Can you imagine his frustration? Today, if there is drug addiction in these institutions as is reported, it is because largely of the frustrations to which the student community is exposed. The standards of perfection that they are supposed to attain, mostly inhuman, unnecessary. Forget the inhuman aspect—unnecessary. I mean, nobody can drink 100% pure distilled water, everybody knows this. Mere tyros in chemistry know this. You need a little impurity in things. I am not suggesting that we have to be impure, but we don't have to have this *asuric* fascination with perfection.

If you remember the story of the *amritamanthan*: the asuras and the devas on one side churning away the ocean of milk. Who got it, finally? The calm, the peaceful, the God-loving community of devas who were blessed by the Lord. So we have to strive for a sense of balance. Today we are not seeking education! We are seeking rank. We are seeking rank that we may progress in our education, that, too, only for getting a job, making more money, whether it is engineering, education, technology, what have you, with its attendant corruption. When a medical institution can charge thirty thousand American dollars for admission! There are institutions charging that and there are students paying it, at what cost to their parents, we don't know.

So, today society is crystallising into a body, into a corpus of tension-ridden, frustration-ridden individuals. The solution, of course, is before you, that material success is not the be-all and end-all of existence.

In fact, there is no such thing as material success. Anybody is successful who can fill his belly, look after his family with average goodwill, love, affection, give them shelter that is necessary, feed them as necessary, clothe them as necessary. Beyond that, when we go into the economic circumstances, banking and building up a big balance, and then along comes a Gorbachev or somebody in China and he is shaking the universe by its roots, and you don't know what is going to happen to our investments and our savings. You say, "What the hell is happening here? I have spent so many miserable years in school, in college. My parents are miserable because they had to mortgage their existence to educate me and now my education, or my existence is tottering because of some fellows here and some there in different corners of the world who are threatening the stability, not only the stability, the existence of this world." All because everybody is seeking power, prominence, ultimacy in the material world. I mean, this is a thesis which hardly needs defending. I am just placing it before you to lay some sort of foundation that a time has come when we must realise that there are two ways of achievement: the internal, the external. We do things for two things which we have already forgotten. One is to get, the other is to become.

I have been dwelling on this for the past few talks I have been giving all over India, that we have to **become** something, is different from we have to **get** something. Getting something is to exist, becoming something is for our emancipation. The problem with education is that these two have become confused, that the getting and the becoming have become confused. Education is supposed to make us be something, become something. We should be educated, not well employed or this, that, and the other. That is a consequence.

So I think we should now carefully distinguish between these two ways: becoming, getting or achieving. Both are essential. Please don't think that I am trying to negate one at the cost of the other, because then I would be belying the teaching that I have received from my guru. The crux of the

143

situation is that either we do this or we do this. Our ancient heritage in India is a clear pointer to the fact that they negated totally the material existence, become recluses, went into jungles. They may have become rishis and mahatmas, but it did nothing for the good of the people.

We today are making the opposite mistake for going totally for the material welfare, material satisfaction, material universe. My Master says, "Balance both." Happiness is more internal than external, and when we think that external things can bring us happiness—perhaps temporarily, yes. But you know how fleeting it is. An ice cream eaten by a child, for the moment it is an ecstasy. Next moment, it's lost. A balloon for which the child on the beach craves. You buy it for two rupees, and the fellows are cheating you, left and right because you are on the beach, and the child is weeping. One stray bit of sand or something comes and the exploded balloon puts the child into tears. So when we look to the material life for our inner satisfaction, for our inner balance, for a sense of contentment, it cannot exist. Temporarily, yes! Permanently, no!

So if you want to seek happiness, we don't say stop earning money, or stop becoming professors, or stop doing research. We say, "Go ahead, but at the same time do something for your internal self. Look inside also. Create something there which will hold you, which will sustain you, not only through this life, but through the hereafter." So we are not asked to renounce anything. You are not asked to renounce education or the high standard of living which some of us may be used to. The *jhopari* man is welcome to stay in his *jhopari*, the palatial man is welcome to stay in his palace. Both have to seek happiness inside. Otherwise, the king is miserable in his palace, the *jhopari* dweller is miserable in his *jhopari*. Both are equally miserable. For misery, there is no categorisation that there is a kingly misery and a beggarly misery. When you cut your finger, both have the same pain. When you suffer from cancer both have the same problems of not merely physical suffering but the mental suffering associated with it. The terminal state which you are anticipating, and by anticipation it becomes more and more potently disastrous for us, destroys our peace of mind first, and then the peace of mind of the family.

So yoga is not only something we have to do, it is something we must do at all cost. This is what I am trying to put before you, that without sacrificing anything that you are doing, without stopping anything that you are doing, continuing to do it in the future better and better, if you also take up the inner way, spending a modicum of your daily time, about one and a half hours, we are able to establish an inner harmony and peace which is independent of our external circumstances. They go on in their way, this goes on this way, very much like the roots of a tree go downwards and downwards, the branches goes upwards and upwards; they are in different directions, but there is harmony between the two. Without the roots the tree cannot exist, without the branches it may.

So this is the broad foundation for the need to meditate, and I wish to assure you again there is no conflict between science and mysticism, or science and spirituality. They are two ways of looking at this universe, two ways of experiencing this universe, two ways of mastering this universe—not conquering this universe, mastering this universe. There is a difference between conquest and mastery. No master has ever conquered anything. Conquests are at the cost of destruction, ravage, and misery. I mean, most of you scientists know today, what you call the rape of Nature! How you are taking out from Nature, more and more what you call irreplaceable resources and are suffering the consequences: pollution of the atmosphere, glaciers melting, the carbon monoxide and the carbon-dioxide in the atmosphere, the greenhouse effect, all miserable things before you, which at any moment can snuff out our existence. Some people may ask, "Do you mean to say that by a few of you meditating, you are going to change the world?" Why not? I mean, one Madam Curie found radium with which today so many cancer patients are being cured. Thousands of them, hundreds of thousands of them. A fellow with a key attached to his kite—electricity! And today you have the marvels of electricity here, right here. It's always one who shows the way. It is useful if others follow behind him. If they don't follow that is lost. There are many ancient traditions which speak of the fact that all these glories and marvels of scientific and technological developments were there centuries before. Those of you who are willing to believe in Atlantus and things like that, and the proof of this is not so much in the factual evidence, but in the philosophical theories that we believe in, the cyclical nature of things. Day follows night,

night follows day. So periods of illumination follow periods of darkness and ignorance. This has been the course through the past several centuries. You can trace it in history. You can trace it in religion.

So if you believe that, and as we use illumination, artificial illumination to turn night into day for our limited purpose, is it not possible to turn this ignorance into illumination again for our purpose and spread that light elsewhere? So, that is the next step that we start yoga, meditation, for our individual growth and development. But nothing is individual. This is one thing we don't appreciate. My Master used to say, you can have a river flowing through your garden. It is your river, but you cannot dam it up and stop the water from flowing to others. They will break your dam. 'They' meaning everybody who is not accessible to that water. Similarly, the wealthy people make the mistake of hoarding the money for themselves. The intelligentia also make this mistake. They form their own secret societies and exchange research notes excluding the public, some under the assumption that the public are always ignorant. They won't understand the arcane mysteries of science, but when are you going to educate them? If you read some of the science fiction stories, of how this crystallisation of the elite eventually pushes them underground, because the earth's surface is full of so-called brutes; they have to hide themselves, build citadels around themselves. Slowly we see this happening nowadays. The distinction between an IIT boy and the rest of the university education. It is a citadel-isation that for the moment you have advantages in campus recruitment, and so on and so forth, is only a sign of the decadence of the times. It shows that we have too little expertise available, therefore, the law of demand and supply is operating, and you are making hay while the sun is shining.

I don't see how an arts graduate is less than a technology graduate or a science graduate or a medical graduate. It is like saying that this hand is better than this hand. If it is true, there is something seriously wrong with it. If one eye sees better than the other you have to go to the ophthalmologist. If one ear hears better than the other you have to go to the ENT surgeon. How can one arm of society claim to be the elite and not another, without facing a similar situation, that in the total body of manhood or humanity there is something seriously wrong. All is not well in the state of Denmark, if you remember your *Macbeth*! *Hamlet* or *Macbeth*, I don't remember.

So, we have to have not only integrated balanced development of the individual, it must eventually contribute to integrated balanced development of society. Every rich man knows that if his house is the only rich house and he is surrounded by poor people, he has to build taller and taller walls every year. He has to have barred gates. He has to have watchman, because the eyes of all the poor people are there. So you see, we have to create a society where a man may earn billions, but he must distribute something of it to everybody else. Like my Master said, if a river runs through your house, take as much water as you want but let the rest flow; as much water as you need, in fact, because my Master was carefully distinguishing between needs and wants. Needs are fundamental to existence; wants are our creation.

So these are some of the basic, structural points of the yogic science with which we are dealing, which is also yogic art, and which I had to learn at the feet of my divine Master. The same teaching we are offering to everybody who is willing to try it. Poor people come easily because they need relief. You know its like a very sick man who goes to hospital, quite easily, without having to be persuaded. But one who has a secret or hidden sickness is not so willing to go to a hospital. He says, *"Kya jaldi hai,* we'll see tomorrow. We'll see day after tomorrow," and then it's too late.

We have really serious problems inside! Like we look into the mirror to look at the blemishes on our skin, if you would only care to look once inside, you will find out what—I can't find a better word than saying, 'wealth of misery' we have got inside; enormous assets of misery which we are trying to work off in our frustration, in our hatred, in our antagonisms, in our suspicion, in our distrust. That is why most people are afraid to meditate. You know, there are many people who are willing to meditate but they are afraid to meditate because, to see the reality that is within, of which we have some suspicion in our conscious state—it's a frightening thing. There have been people who have sat to meditate before my Master, and after three minutes they have got out, shrieking out of that and saying, "I cannot stand it. I cannot tolerate it." This is the horror in all those who become addicted to drugs, who go into themselves in a different way. The 'snake pit', one of the old famous English films, which showed this sort of decadence where the inner self is so disastrous, so dangerous, so frightening that we dare not look inside. Then you find insomnia, you find inability to sleep, not being able to be alone, always seeking company. Man was not meant to be in groups. He always stood alone. That is why you find at the summit of achievement, whether in science or in arts or literature or in spirituality, the top is a lonesome place. In material achievement, the top **is** very much a lonesome place because they have nothing to look inside to, for assistance, for help, for companionship. It has always been a mystery how the spiritual giants of this world went off into deserts, mountaintops, and they were quite happy there. They did not need company, they did not need service, they did not need assistance, no friendship, because they had Him whom you call God, whom we call Master, right there inside and He was always available. This is the most important step in spirituality, that from outside reference libraries, external sources of advice, external sources of assistance, fire service, medical service, insurance, etc., you put all your dependence into one Person, with a capital 'P', right here in the heart whom you call the *Antaryaamin nivasin* of every creative being, in religion—He who is present in the heart of every creative being, says the Gita. And then, when you are able to associate with him, connect with him, refer to him, hear his voice, little by little, progressively we find that His companionship is not only enough, it's more than enough. His guidance is all.

The story of Arjuna and Parthasarathi, Krishna is only an epitomisation, an illustration of this inner connection, that here was the soul prepared to hand over the reins of its existence to the Master of that soul, the Krishna of that episode. And he was happy, he was victorious. Initially he rebelled. You all know how much he rebelled. "No, no, I cannot shoot. I cannot shoot at my own relations. There is the great grandfather of mine; there are my elder brothers," etc. You have been watching this. And Krishna says, "Who do you think they are? Yours?" When you come to the last or nearly the last episode of Karna, where Karna is killed and Arjuna for a moment boasts, "At last I have killed him," Krishna comes down and for once he is harsh with Arjuna. He says, "You killing Karna? Who are you to kill Karna? At least eight people have killed him already. Indra, when came in the garb of a Brahmin and took away his *kavacha* and his *kundala*. His mother Kunti, who came to him and took a promise that he would not kill his brothers. Then somebody else, then somebody else. His Guru Parashurama who cursed him that at the moment of need you would not have this power.

So, we don't kill, we don't create. The ultimate truth is that everything is done there; we are an instrument through which these things happen. Now it requires a great deal of humility to accept it. It is always nice to feel that "I have succeeded. I am a gold medallist. I belong to IIT. I have got this job. I am the professor. I am the whatever it is!" Now, achievement would be worthless without this egocentric attitude to it. One who cannot say **I** achieved it, for him success has no meaning; for one who cannot say that this is **my** wealth, wealth has no meaning. Therefore, religion, great yogic systems, great teachers have said the **I** and the **my** are the two things we have to cut out of our existence. Because so long as the **I** is there, I am prone to say 'I', 'I', 'I', 'I'. So long as the **my** is there, 'mine', 'mine', 'mine', 'mine'. Now how to do this? If you try to be non-egotistic, to become humble—in South India, we have this ancient but rather stupid tradition where we build our doors four and a half feet high so that everybody has to go down like this [bending] and they claim it promotes humility. It only promotes knocked heads and curses on our ancestors. So that every time you knock you head you say, "Which damn fool built this house?" And it's your grandfather or your great grandfather. Humility cannot be taught by artificial means. Humility has to come, not by throwing away the ego, which is one fundamental teaching of our system of Sahaj Marg, that without the ego we cannot exist. My Master used a very simple example. He said, "If I feel I can lift this table, it is my ego which speaks, 'I can lift this table'." So it is necessary, but it has to be refined to such a level where when I say 'I', as my Master beautifully said once in Copenhagen: "When I say 'I', I don't know whether it refers to this being or to my Master or to God." We have to use something. You cannot say "table lifted." Then you'll ask, "Who?"

You know grammar: *Kartaa, Karma, Karana Sampradaana,* and all this nonsense. We are bound by·our grammar as much by our science and as much by our technology. We have to say, "Who did it? What are you? Who was your parent?" But we have known ancient traditions that a great boy went to a guru and he said, "Who are your parents, what is your *gotra?*" He said, "I'll find out. I don't know." He went to his mother and she was an honest lady, pure in the sense that she could tell the truth and she said, "My son, I don't know, because when I was a servant maid, I have served so many people and I don't know who is your father." The boy went and told this to the guru, potential guru. He said, "You have spoken the truth, you are my *chela.*"

So, we have great traditions like this which are supposed to support us. Dharma means that which upholds. Without something to uphold you, you have nothing. Even this much wanted intellectual education. You need a university, you need professors. They are the foundation on which the alumnae stands, the professors themselves stand, and those are the creation of grants and gifts. So if you go back like this there is no room for pride and arrogance, in that, "I did this, I did this, I did this." But as I repeat, it is very difficult to do this, because it's like removing a tree, leaf by leaf. By the time you have removed one side, the other side is growing again.

Yogic practice says, start thinking of Him, only think of Him, remember Him, and then you will automatically find that now everything you do, everything you think, you are automatically attributing to Him. Like a child says, "My father bought this." He doesn't have to think. The child in that sense is egoless, at the age of three and a half, four, five. My father bought this. This is my booty. Who bought it? My father bought this. Who cooked *'paneer matar'* today? My mother cooked. The child is proud to ascribe doership, the *kartritva* to somebody else, but when we lose that childish innocence, childlike innocence, we need to feel that I have done this. Who made this? I made this. Oh! Did you really make it? No, no, I shelled the peas, therefore, I made *'paneer matar'*. Well, for children it's alright, but when you are an adult, to claim that "I did this, I did this, I did this," you know it's as stupid as Arjuna saying, "I killed Karna," and he was scolded by Krishna who said, "At least eight people have killed him before you fired the arrow that finally finished him."

Now here I want to come to another important point: dharma. Many people say, "I am leading a dharmic life. I have donated so much to charity. I have never done anything wrong. Why should I meditate?" There is one aspect of Karna's end which I think many people have not understood. See, when he is knocked out from his chariot, lethally wounded, unable to die because the *dharmamaataa, dharmadevataa* comes and protects him. Krishna, of course the all knower, the divine, the ultimate, comes around, changes himself into a Brahmin, and says, "Your last act of *dharma* on earth, please do now."

He says, "I have nothing left. I am dying."

He says, "No, you have all the *karmaphala* of your dharma. Give that to me." And he does that. With a little bit of water, he says, "Take it. All the fruits of dharma, I give you." Then only he was able

154

to die. *Adharma* he has got rid of. What is the use of dharma, if he could not die peacefully? And Krishna had to show him the way. "Idiot, don't bank on dharma or adharma. Give up both. You have given up adharma, now give up dharma. Give it to me. I am the only person who can hold dharma and yet continue."

So this fallacy that, "I am leading a dharmic life, therefore, I'll have *mukti*" is wrong, because my Master said that if you led a dharmic life, you come again into a better existence, but you would surely come back. The difference between good and bad, evil and vice, virtue and these things, is only in the nature of rebirth that you are going to get. For *mukti* you have to give up both—*sukha dukhe same kritvaa laabha alaabhau jaya ajayau*—all this the Gita says, and we are doing *paarayana* but not understanding what it really means. This is the danger, this is the misery in which we have been plunged by superficial knowledge of anything. Half knowledge is dangerous, says the old proverb. Here we have less than half knowledge. We hear something of the Gita on the loudspeaker or scene from the Gita and we are satisfied that today's job is over. The Gita itself spoils our future by saying, one who reads it wholly everyday will get such and such a *phalashruti*, they call it. One who reads only nine *adhyaayas* will get so much, one *adhyaaya* so much, one *shloka* so much. I mean, it's crazy! It's like giving a child a bit of chocolate to make it sit down and study. But we adults take the chocolate for achievement and say, "I have studied the Gita."

So dharma is no guarantee, I mean it is not at all anything to do with mukti! Right living, right thinking, right attitude to life are enjoined upon us by the fact of our human birth, nothing more. That I do right is not something which even deserves encomium from the public. That I don't do wrong is not praiseworthy. As my Master said again and again, human being is differentiated from the rest of existence—animals, insects, birds, plants, everything—by possessing two attitudes which they don't have: the intellect and the will. The intellect to help you to decide what is right, the will to enable you to do what is right. Now most of us know what is right and what is wrong, but that we continue to do what is wrong is only showing a lack of will power.

Therefore, what is necessary is not puritive clinics and therapies, but something to strengthen will power and there again meditation helps, because you sit quietly in a particular pose, trying to restrain all outer tendencies, turning your mind upon himself. This very efforts strengthens mind progressively day after day and therefore, the mental power which you call will power. Then how can such a person succumb to other things outside himself? I think succumbing is the fact of our existence. We succumb to temptations, we succumb to opportunities. Sometimes we don't know why we change jobs even. "Oh! I thought it was a better job, it offered a few hundred rupees more," which is only a temptation. Are you doing something better or are you only earning something more? Today, earning something more has become the *summum bonum* of existence. Having something more is again the flamboyant ways of living: possession, bigger houses, bigger cars. It has become the *summum bonum* because it is an externalisation of inner achievement, and those who flaunt it are suspicious of this and they have to show off that they are living happily. "Well, I have achieved. This is my symbol of success."

Now to cut off all these things, we very much need to go into meditation, get the inner balance, strengthen our mind, progressively develop will power, associate ourselves with Him who is inside, which is but myself: my **self**. This hiatus, this divorce between the inner self and the external self is what, for instance, schizophrenia is all about. Psychologists may call it something else—divided self. What is a divided self? It doesn't exist in the brain. Psychologists may deal with the brain, but the brain is not the cause. There is something fundamental. What is behind human misery? It can be so many things for so many different people. Not marrying the girl he loves for a boy, not getting the job he wants when he is out of college, not getting the payment that other people get in similar jobs, third one; not having the house which the other people have, fourth one. It goes on multiplying. As you go higher and higher, our greed for advancement, possessions, earnings grows in some sort of progression. I don't remember the progression.

So this is the tragedy of existence and therefore, my Master used to say very wisely, but I thought in those days, you know, that it was not so wise, that the unsuccessful people are more happy than the successful people because they have learnt to .live with un-success. The poor man is more contented. You see the people in *dehat*. They are setting their *charpays*, smoking their *chillums*, singing some song, they are happy. They are facing misery, they are facing possible death. If there is no monsoon they are dead. But they are happy. The people in their plenty are miserable. They cannot sleep, they cannot be alone, they cannot eat, they are afraid of pollution, corruption, this, that, and the other—filtered water, purified foodstuffs, packaged goods.

The way to get rid of all this is not by the external idea of education that we are rolling out in our universities or school or colleges. It is necessary, it is very valuable, it is a must. We should not at this stage make the mistake of our ancestors, of becoming recluses and walking off into the jungle and negating one half of life. We have to learn now to do the way they did, retaining the way we are doing things, bringing both into a harmony, which is a must.

Now most of the science literature that you read nowadays are modern books by popular science writers, who are trying to bring together mysticism and science. There are umpteen books today, which shows you the non-material nature of the material universe. You don't have to be a physicist to understand or a mathematician. I don't know mathematics at all, but I enjoy these books. They are saying the same things that our ancient Vedic rishis have said, that "In the heart of matter there is nothing but **Me**," the Lord says. And today you find, you go through the atom, the nucleus, and to the sub-nuclear particles, and you are going on and on and on and they are breeding like guinea pigs. I don't know what is the current tally, 128 basic particles, or something like that, but it would soon be 256, or 512. You know, its like the last prime number by a computer. You'll never get to the last one because if mathematics says that the series is infinite, where does the last prime number exist? It is futile to use a computer, a valuable computer, to get the next prime number, the highest prime number and spend three and a half years, as was reported for the last prime number. What for? It is an achievement. He found the last prime number. Okay. What did he achieve? How has it helped humanity? So even in research they are stupid avenues of research which may find something but of no use to us, like the last prime number. Somebody else will find the next one. Seven years of computer time.

We must know what we need. We must know where to look for it. How to find it? When found, how to use it? Without this basic wisdom our life will be shattered, whatever be the superficial success.

Yoga makes it possible for all of us to achieve this precisely because we are able to now at least attempt to balance the inner and the outer. Without the one we have not the other. Every saint has said when you build a house you create an inside and an outside. By creating the walls I have, of course, a beautiful amphitheatre here. But it is illuminated inside; it is dark outside. Some child may be afraid to go out now. When you close the doors you are afraid that somebody will try to open it. As my Master said, "When you lock the door, remember you lock yourself in as much as you lock others out." So success locks us in and everybody else out. But when you go inside and you have this inner success, which is intangible, which is not visible, on which nobody can lay hands, nobody can rob you of, even death cannot deprive you of it, then there is something permanent to hold on to.

It is the impermanence of things which makes us frightened. The loss of wealth is not something that we are afraid of because if you are young enough, you can create it all over again. It is the impermanence. Like today's budget, we don't know what happened this evening. Most of these people here are afraid of the budget. They have had an inkling in the railway budget, the telecommunication changes. It is going to erode all your effort, but they forget that government can only nibble, like rabbits at grass. One natural cataclysm and everything is wiped off. Therefore, we are afraid of wars, we are afraid of nuclear bombs, atomic bombs, neutron bombs, all these things that are going to come in the hereafter.

Somebody was saying yesterday that in the Gita, in the *mahabharata mahayudha*, eighteen days warfare, eighteen crore people were killed. I don't know where he found this statistic, but if that was the case of the wars of those times, can you imagine what will be the consequence of the next war if it comes, God forbid.

It is very heartening to find that politics in Europe has made such drastic changes in the last one year. In a sense the fear of war is receding, but that is also one man. It is not a committee of nations or Nobel Prize winners. It was one head of state who had the guts to face death every morning at the hands of the very instruments of destruction that his own government created, and he is still alive. God bless him.

So, we need great men to do great things, but we need lesser men to achieve them or help them to achieve these things, and in turn to achieve it for themselves. If he brings peace for his country, we are enjoying the peace, but we must allow that peace to last. If the sweeper comes and cleans the streets, we must keep the streets clean by not washing everything out of the house and throwing it on the pavement. Our Indian culture is inner cleanliness and outside dirt. The Western culture is outside cleanliness and inner dirt. Now we have to bring the two together, inner cleanliness and outer cleanliness. So wherever you look, it is the same story—unbalance or imbalance between the inner and the outer.

Yoga, let me assure you, is the only way, because it is the only way of going inwards. Education is teaching you some facts, as somebody once told me. One of my professors in BHU said, "Science can tell you how it happened, but not why it happened." Now we very much want to know why things happen. Where everything fails until you go inwards. Therefore, the 'how' here, the 'why' here, and when the two are in balance, we are able to transcend both and say, "Well, let it be in its place. I am rising beyond both."

So this is the spiritual adventure in which we invite all of you to initially participate, prove for yourself that there is something in it, not test it, like eating *paneer matar* once and saying it is good. It is a process you have to undergo, like education. Every child is against education. You know with how much love you have to chaperon your little child to the KG class. You have to give it sweets, you have to pet it, you have to love it—*nahi, nahi, beta kuchh nahi wahan khatra nahi, hum aajayenga tumhe le jayange,* all these sort of things. It's a process, and then when it starts appreciating what education is doing for it and if it falls in love with education, now you cannot keep him away from school.

So it needs time. Everything needs time. We have a story in Tamil Nadu that a lady could not have a child, and a guru told her to go around a *vata vriksha* nine times every day, and she went around it nine times and started feeling her belly. Children are not born in that way. They need time. Conception followed by growth in the foetus, followed by delivery, coming out, being separated from the mother.

Yoga begins in the mother's womb, where the baby to be born and the mother are one. Then comes this enormous trauma of birth, as they call it, when the child is born into the external world and it is alone. Inside, it was dark but perfectly happy. Outside, it is light but miserable. Therefore the baby weeps. This separation of the mother and the child, of the intellect and the heart, everywhere it is happening all the time, but of course we have to be born, like we have to be born in this world also. We have to be born into the world of knowledge. We have to be born into the world of wealth, but as philosophy says, he who is reborn a second time in this life is the spiritualist, the yogi, the abhyasi, because he has literally a new birth into a new existence, not forgetting the human aspect, living very much as a human being. Our marg is the *grihastha* marg. We have no truck with sanyasa. We have no truck with renunciation, throwing off our responsibilities and walking off as if it is only I who matter. It is irresponsible behaviour. It's cowardly. We live a perfectly human satisfied life in all its aspects, but in the right way, normalising our activities in all fields, even sex. My Master said, "God is not a fool to create sex and then ask you to live a celibate life." We have no truck with celibacy either, but it does not mean license. We are always swinging from one extreme to the other extreme like a pendulum. A moment of frustration, a moment of joy. A moment of vice, a moment of repentance. Smaller vice; ultimately the pendulum has to come to rest sometime.

While talking of pendulums, I am reminded of a fact. When I started this talk I told you we have to unbecome what we are. When you wind the clock, it is the unwinding of the spring which runs the clock, not your winding of the spring. Please remember that.

I invite you all, with my Master's grace, his mercy, to try this method, do it for a few months, see it for yourself, and I am sure you will have to continue beyond that, because it is the way which will balance your inner and external lives, bringing a satisfaction and a contentment which by and large we need today.

Thank you.

Memories

Dear Brothers & Sisters,

It has been a very happy occasion to come here. I wish it had been a longer stay but this is Babuji's permission, that one and a half days is enough; that this is possible is due to the kindness of Brother Kashiram Agarwalji who is able to do all the arrangements in such a short time. I had hoped to be able to stay here longer and visit some nearby centres. May be it will be possible another time.

On this trip I had visited two centres in Bihar, the Calcutta centre, and also Kanpur, Allahabad. Unfortunately, due to a little indisposition, I could not go to Gorakhpur as planned. But I am happy to see brothers and sisters from so many centres in Uttar Pradesh here. I am told that nearly 600 people have come, which is very good.

I am pleased to see that there are signs of better and better discipline at our meetings, more brotherhood and a deeper sense of association with Sahaj Marg. All these things are growing which is a sign of definite progress towards the goal. I remember, in Shahjahanpur, even during Babuji's lifetime, the centre was only, what we say, *'nam ke vaste'* centre, few people. It was all tonnes of people coming from outside and it was always for me something un-understandable that where Babuji Maharaj was sitting, there are twenty abhyasis

Talk at Shahjahanpur on 25 March, 1990

belonging to one or two families. But now we see when preceptors are active how much work can be really done

Today one of our abhyasis, a young lady, was suggesting that perhaps because we don't have the possession or the ability to enter our ashram in Shahjahanpur, we have been holding celebrations all over the country. I think it is a good thing, because had we been confined only to Shahjahanpur, I don't think the Mission would have grown so much in the last seven or eight years. That it is growing very fast, you can all see. In every centre there is growth and I am glad that it is not only growth in numbers, there is also growth in quality. When you see the new preceptors list, you will be astonished that there are so many preceptors in India. It is not that preceptors make the growth, or whoever does it. It shows the increasing need for more and more people at more and more centres, because there are more and more abhyasis everywhere.

It is Babuji's wish that we should look to quality and not to quantity. Many people use this quotation in the wrong way and try to keep the number as limited, pretending that if there are few numbers, the quality will automatically increase. Six rotten tomatoes in a basket will not become six good tomatoes. At the same time, Babuji has said so many times, that it was his *gurudakshina*, his vow to his Master Lalaji Maharaj that this system should spread throughout the world, which means that there has to be a geographical growth and a growth in numbers, too. When Babuji Maharaj said this shall be the sole way of practice within the next twenty years, it means most of humanity will have to follow this system, which means numbers. Why I am saying this is, we should all be prepared to serve. It is not enough to just come and sit in our satsangh, take the benefit and go home better in spirituality. Of course, that is what you come for, but the second aspect is your willingness to serve the Master from whom you receive so much, to serve the Mission from which you have received so much, to propagate the Method which has raised you to levels of spirituality which you could not have dreamt of earlier. So, it is a sacred duty that is cast upon all of us, not just a *gururina* or a *guru dakshina*. It is a duty.

I wonder how many of you will be able to shoulder this, or be willing to shoulder this responsibility, because it is indeed a responsibility. I find that the younger generation is very staunch in their devotion. They have been deeply steeped in Sahaj Marg. Most of them are more idealistic, which is to be expected of the younger generation. They are more forward in their approach to the system and to the guide. They are more patient, and at the same time they are more demanding. Youth has a way of extracting what it needs from the elder generations of the society, which is a good thing. When youth stops making such demands upon us, we will just rot away.

So it is to the youth that we look for regeneration of society. They are the future of our race, not only the future of the society in which we are embedded today. If one generation of youth falls,

167

there is no next generation of youth, no next generation of humanity. But at the same time, they need to channelise their enthusiasm, their need for the perfect fruitful life. They have to be guided in these endeavours by the elder generation, who must follow or keep pace with the youth in this matter, because with increasing age, we tend to become more and more compromising in our attitudes to values, in our attitudes to demands, in our attitudes to needs, and we say, "Well, you know, we cannot change everything all at once! Let them do it."

So, I believe that, in society, today, as we go along into the tomorrows of the future, it is to the youth that we must look for direction and it is to the elder generation that we must turn for steam-power. Both have a part to play, vital parts to play. Both must balance their existence. One in providing the necessary motivation, as is modernly called today: giving guidance, giving youthfulness, giving buoyancy, giving of their vitality, giving of their immense longing for spirituality and values of Reality, and look to the elder generation for guidance, to tame these values into the right proportion, not to destroy them, but to tame them so that they can be used like we tame electricity to the acceptable voltage.

Some people have been talking of memories when they come to Shahjahanpur. We all have memories, not only of Shahjahanpur, but elsewhere, too. Memories can be destructive, memories can be constructive, memories can be weak, memories can strengthen us, memories can make us weak, memories can make us joyful. There is nothing in memory itself. It is what we make of memories, like everything else in this world. I have seen people coming and sitting here and just weeping at the memory of the Master. I think it is a little weak. It is weak emotions. I remember, once Babuji Maharaj was going from Madras by train. He was seated in the compartment by the Grand Trunk Express. There were fifty or sixty people outside, including the indomitable, formidable Dr. Varadachari, and he was weeping. I mean, Dr. Varadachari pretending to have a cold, wiping his eyes and sniffing so that people should not see that it was really emotion. Babuji was sitting cool and collected. I went to him. I said, "Babuji, so many people are weeping. How is it you have no tears in your eyes? Have you no emotion at all?" Babuji looked very compassionate. He said there is a time for tears. When you begin your sadhana there is a need for emotion, to show that your heart is indeed responding to this treatment that we call Sahaj Marg. But if you continue to weep, it will weaken you. It will make you useless. So even the memories of the Master that we have, if they are not used in the right way, they just deteriorate into emotional mush.

I must caution all of you into how we use, how we formulate these memories for ourselves, so that the Master, even as a memory, can help us in our growth. I see people talking of those days when Babuji used to stoop and pick up pieces of *kuda* from the pathways in Shahjahanpur in his ashram and put them into the *kudapatra*. How many of us are doing it here? The memory is no use, unless you do it, and if you have such venerable and venerated memories of your Master that you keep talking about him all the time, how he did not allow wastage of food, how when he saw a tap running he would go, close the tap, if we do not use these memories as living examples of a Master who was, who is, and who shall always be our guide, what is the use of such memories?

Unfortunately, I am not willing to praise people who have great memories of their Master and do nothing about it. It is too easy to talk of memories, too easy to weep at the microphone, too easy to beat one's breast and say there can be none other than him. It is a denial of the truth for which he lived. It is the denial of the truth by which he left this earth, that every one can be like Him, must be like Him, should try to be like Him, otherwise Sahaj Marg is a failure.

It is said that if one human being can do anything in any field, whether it is sports, adventure, yoga, it only shows that other people can also do it. Now in the physical field, not all can do it, because there are physical limitations, but in spirituality there are no limitations, and if, you know, we are going to confuse humility with abject weakness and say, "No, no, I can never be like Him," it is like the lion's cub saying, "I can never be a lion." I see these *Sardarjis*, our Sikh brothers and sisters, I have been very familiar with them in the days when I had to go to the Punjab frequently on my business travels. A tiny Sikh child of three years is no less than a grown up Sikh in its approach to life, in its bravery. It is prepared to go and fight twenty people, if necessary, because the Sikh father says, "*Sher de puttar, ja*". "You are my child. You are a tiger's cub, how can you be weak?" I have never seen a single Sikh child of any age daunted by elders. I was once travelling from Shahjahanpur to Bareilly on my way back to Delhi and I saw one single truck full of sugarcane and one beardless *sardar* driving, probably eighteen or nineteen. His truck had broken down. He was undaunted; there was no worry on his face. People were stopping to help him. He said "*Koi bat nahin.*" He was not afraid of the darkness, he was not afraid of dacoits, he was not afraid of being alone.

So, this is the sort of breed that you must breed, in spirituality at least, and when we have the Master who says this is a method by which everyone can become like this, must become like this, it is possible. My Master did it before me, I have done it, and now you shall do it. When Babuji says these things and we sit and wail and weep and we say, "No, no, no, once and for all it is over," don't you think we should be ashamed of such talk? It would be a denial of all the love, of all the sacrifice that that poor old man whom we call the Master made for us. Let us not betray him by stupid, illogical, assumed humility. I would rather try to be a lion and fail and become at least a tiger than assume I can be nothing better than a goat and remain a pig, perhaps. I believe that whatever my Master said was true. If he said it is possible, it must be possible. If he said it shall be, it shall be. If he said, "Do it, I take responsibility," he **will** take responsibility. But we come to these preconceived notions of false humility with which Hinduism has condemned us to one of the worst existences on earth: hypocrisy in language, hypocrisy in behaviour and we go around saying, "*Nahin, nahin, yeh to mumkin nahin hai, bhai! Ek hi to ho sakta hai; woh to saheb ajeeb the, laajavab the, ek hi to aisa ho sakte hai, hum kya ho sakte hai*"!

Shame on such talk. I for one cannot condone, cannot countenance such weakness, whether real or assumed. If it is real, you can be helped; if it is assumed, may Master help you and pardon you.

So memories must be strengthening us. A memory is a foundation laid in the past for the future. Every day we are creating more memories. What is life but creation of memories, in one way if you look at it. Everything that we do, everything that we enjoy, everything that we suffer becomes a memory. In our old days we cannot act, we depend on our memories to fill our lonely days and hours and nights, but if they are properly used, though the events themselves disappear like the foundations of a building which go underground, yet they are there, firm enough to support the superstructure which is there for you to see. So let us not talk futilely, emotionally, wistfully, wishfully of dreams, of memories, of the greatness of the Master. I charge you all with not talking of the greatness of the Master, unless you are willing to stand up and emulate His greatness. Otherwise our life is a lie.

I don't believe in the greatness of one man who is our leader not filtering down to us, however weakly it is filtered. You see a sugarcane juice-*wala*. He pushes through the sugarcane twenty times through the some pair of rolls and he is extracting up to the last drop of juice that is there in the sugarcane; and we have the man whom we call the Master, who is supposed to be a Special Personality, than whom there was never any greater, and we are satisfied with just sitting in meditation and getting rid of our problems of life, getting rid of our headaches, getting rid of the so called *pretas and bhutas* in our homes. Is this what spirituality is for?

You know, preceptors especially have a big responsibility. I am not happy with the way preceptors handle their responsibilities. It is not just enough to just do a little cleaning and give a little transmission and note it down in the record that today I gave sittings to eight people. I believe it is the preceptors who must beware of numbers. One sitting well given, properly handled, one abhyasi properly disposed of, strengthened in his every fibre of his being when he goes out of your house, is better than twenty weaklings. We must put our heart into it. We must put our life into it. A life of a preceptor is a job of dedication, of love: love of the Master, dedication to the Master. We love him so much, we are dedicated to him so much, that we cannot lose an opportunity presented to us by an abhyasi to show our love and devotion to the Master. This should be the attitude, not that we have corrected this tendency in the abhyasi and that tendency in somebody else. If our preceptors put their shoulders to the wheel, Sahaj Marg shall spread over this whole universe. If they are satisfied with scratching the surface and doing their modicum of duty, because of duty and not because

173

of love of the Master, it shall be what it is or not even so much in the future. It is a lie to say that Babuji Maharaj has laid the foundation for the next ten thousand years; it is a lie to say that it will grow by itself; it is a lie to say that he has charged such and such a place for ten thousand years, so we don't need anything else. These are all lies. Everything has to be maintained. If he has built, we have to maintain. If he has created, we have to maintain that creation, give it more impetus, push it onwards and onwards into bigger dimensions, higher dimensions of growth. It is not something very easy but at the same time it is unimaginably easy, because once a car has started, it is not necessary to push it anymore. It moves now on its own momentum. But until that stage comes, we have to put our shoulders to the wheel.

So to just sit back complacently and say, "No, no, no! He has done everything, it cannot be otherwise." I have heard people talking of the Shahjahanpur ashram, that Babuji has charged it for ten thousand years, not caring to think that this building will never stand a thousand years. It is, after all, built of brick and stone. If it stands 500 years, it is still too much, by my estimate. It can, if you do the necessary maintenance. But I don't see anything standing for a thousand years. What he meant was, like what Christ said, "My kingdom is not of this world." This spiritual world that he has created for us! Yes, why ten thousand years, it shall be eternal, but there too, if we are willing to put our shoulders to the wheel and keep pushing. Each generation taking over the responsibility from the previous generation, not allowing things to falter, not allowing things to come to a stop, not allowing things to become weak, diluted, then and only then will this go on and on and on, for eternity. If at any stage it falters... Please! I would like to assure you that it will stop.

So, each generation has a tremendous responsibility to the past because that is where we got this immensely magnificent, superbly efficient, utterly simple system, and to the future, of whom we are the founders, whom we cannot let down, because they are going to be our children and our grandchildren.

So I would like all of you, sisters and brothers, to remember this, that as Babuji used to say, this is not the way of the weak. This is the arena of the lions. We don't want bleating sheep; we don't kill them; we don't eat them. They are welcome, but they come here for their benefit. It is the lions who must roar into the jungle, clear the way for civilised existence, a spiritual existence, and I pray that every one of you will develop a lion's heart, because in you rests the future of the system, the future of the Master's Divine name, and the future of your own posterity.

Thank you.

Simplicity

It's nothing to be surprised at. A real cook knows how long each thing has to be cooked for: potatoes fifteen minutes, meat forty-five minutes, *palak* two minutes. Cooking is an art in which time is important—how long something should be fried? So a cook essentially deals with time. Rest is all addition and subtraction. Removing unwanted waste, adding this and that. That is only to create some fragrance.

Some people are afraid to talk because they don't know how long they can talk. People imagine that a speech should be long. Like many of our abhyasis think that a long sitting is a good sitting and a short sitting is not a good sitting. Actually the opposite is true. The shorter the sitting, the better the sitting, because in my lifetime association with my Master, the greatest sittings were the shortest sittings. And one of them was only forty seconds, about which Babuji himself spoke for years and years. Whenever he met somebody he used to say, "You know that sitting I gave Parthasarathi. It was only forty-five seconds. But you know what I gave in it?" So to give something really valuable—if I want to give two hundred tonnes of sand, you require trucks and lorries and bullock carts and camel carts and probably ten days to transport it. But to give a small diamond weighing twenty-five carats, worth a million rupees, it doesn't take much time. The size is small, the value is enormous; the transmission of object from one hand to another doesn't take any time.

So these two principles are there in cooking-time and in transmission: we try to do away with time as much as possible. Now you can say, "Why do you give forty-five minutes sittings?" It is because in our celebrations it is the principle laid down by my Master that we should have one hour sittings. Because we wait essentially on two occasions: on Basant Panchami day and on Babuji's birthday for grace to descend. And when we wait there can be no time limit. If you have a Master there who is capable of linking grace to the assembly it may happen in the first minute, it may happen in the last minute of the hour; depends on Him. Because, cleaning has to be done, proper atmosphere has to be created, the purity and love have to be brought.

I have often talked of marriage in the West. And you will permit me to speak something about sex? It's a very important subject. Why marriage for sex? It is to create this atmosphere of purity, holiness, where two hearts are united and because the hearts are united, the bodies can unite with absolute freedom—permission from God, permission from society, no guilt. People often say, "What! After all, there is no difference. It's a sheet of paper." It's this sheet of paper which makes all the difference! You go to college, you have a degree. Without that degree on a sheet of paper, you are not a Bachelor of Science or a Bachelor of Arts or a doctor of science. It is a sheet of paper. You go to buy something and they give you a voucher—it is a piece of paper.

177

Without it, if you walk out of the shop with only the things with you and not the paper, they will catch you and say you have robbed it. So, in all cases it is only a sheet of paper which differentiates between legality and illegality, between morality and immorality, between right and wrong. So when in the West people use this piece of paper as something stupid, they are making a great mistake and only satisfying a conscience which is already deeply troubled.

It is necessary in every sphere to bring this dignity into what we are doing. In marriage we have these old customs, ritualistic, which are no longer valid. Why are they not valid? Because people come and some pundit is reciting some nonsense. The girl's parents are busy inviting their guests. The father's parents are busy counting the dowry and the vessels that they are getting. The bride and bridegroom couldn't care less; they are looking at each other shyly or with lust, or whatever it is. So the whole thing is a farce. Today's marriages are farces, in India, in the West, anywhere.

So we are trying to bring in a new type of marriage in our Sahaj Marg *sanstha*. Some people have questioned, "How are you doing these marriages?" I said, "My Master started it. I did not start it." In my Master's lifetime at least seven marriages were performed by Babuji Maharaj himself and in his presence I have performed two marriages. So I had the whole authority of the Master to do it. Why did he do it? Because, he said, "Ritualistic nonsense is a corrupt way. People only want to show off, flaunt their wealth, flaunt their power." One minister comes and everybody is wanting to take pictures with him.

I remember a marriage in south India, in Madras. The girl was one of our abhyasis. The parents were abhyasis. All the sisters were abhyasis. They called a very corrupt minister, a very corrupt immoral fellow, and they gave the *mangalsutra* in his hand and said, "Give this to the bride." At that moment, I said, "This marriage is finished." You could not find a more corrupt person. And the marriage is on the rocks. The girl is divorced. You can say, "How could that happen? Suppose somebody else had given, do you mean to say this would not have happened?" Yes! It wouldn't. If you give a bomb to a child you know what will happen. And if you give it to a technical person who knows what to do with it, there is a difference! You allow a child to have a match box, it can kill itself, it can burn up the house. Isn't it? So who does what is a very important thing. Not every priest who wears white clothes is a moral person or even a religious person. They are also earning a living, that is why they have to go through these colleges of theology and seminaries, equip themselves, get a degree, and then they are given a parish. They go there, earn money, live like kings, live like lords, eating the best food, and on Sundays they preach very sententiously, telling their flock how to live simply. Now when the preacher does not live a simple life, how do you expect his flock to live a simple life?

So there is no example today. Our teachers don't set examples for us. They don't become examples for us worth following. Somebody said, they are always following the Master. Why? Because he is an example. I questioned this idea of love, that everybody loves. It is possible that there is some love in our hearts for the Master. But that there is so much love that we follow, I question. I don't think it is humanly possible for such love to exist so easily, so quickly, without sacrifice.

Today when I went for a walk I was given an example. I was going from Delhi to Bareilly. We had a small problem with the car. We stopped for six hours, so we were reaching Bareilly at 12:30 in the night. There was a whole line of bullock carts, about a hundred and fifty bullock carts, and all the drivers were sleeping covered up to the head. My driver was a *sardarji*. He said, "I want to show you what Uttar Pradesh is." He used to call it *Ulta Pradesh*, meaning 'upside down Pradesh.' He said, "Watch the fun." So he stopped the car, got out, and turned the leading cart out. He just pulled the first bullock this way—U turn—back towards the original state and all the carts turned and followed. Now you cannot say the bullocks are following because they worship or they have respect. It is their tendency to follow. Like you have one duck crossing the street, and all the ducks cross the street. Why, even in human beings, one man yawns, everybody starts to yawn. One man wants to go to the toilet, everybody wants to go to the toilet. Can we say this is because of love or because of respect for the Master?

So coming to this topic of following the Master, simple existence, our friend, our brother, referred to the simplicity of village life. This is a mistaken conception that village people are simple.

Some of them are the most corrupt, and the most mischievous, and the most scheming fellows. I know that in the south, villagers are often criminal, mischievous, and their simplicity is a fraud. They are not simple. They are primitive. Please learn to differentiate between primitive existence and simple existence. Primitive by reason of their primitiveness. They are not changed; over the centuries they have not changed. When Babuji said, "Adopt a simple life for saintliness," well, if all our village people were simple because of their own simplicity, our India should be full of saints today. But it is full of criminals today. Everybody knows it. In villages are criminals, murderers, rapists, dacoits. So what is this simplicity that we are trying to bring?

There is a famous statement, I don't know by whom, perhaps Ralph Waldo Emerson, that simplicity is achieved by giving up complexity. That means we have to be complex first and then become simple. To renounce something, you must have had it first. I cannot renounce wealth which I never had. A man with fifteen rupees in his pocket cannot say, "I have renounced wealth, brother. You see I have been having a very simple existence. I don't wear shirts." He never had anything to renounce. He never had a shirt to take off. He never had water to wash in. He never had a toilet to clean. So what is this renunciation? What is this simplicity? We are fooling people with these villagers and saying, "Look at this simple existence, look at this beautiful life." Because we are complex, we look at it from the other side. The grass is always greener on the other side of the river. So we come for a few days, bathe in cold water, admire the peacocks and then say, "Thank Heavens, it is finished."

Wealth has to be had before it can be renounced. You must have a family before you can renounce the family. You must have bad habits before you give them up. I am not suggesting that you must acquire bad habits before renouncing. The idea of renunciation is: you cannot renounce what you cannot have. Way back in 1958, I was sitting in my office. A big strong swami came. He was from one of these Gouda *mutts*. Nice fellow, well speaking, in English, good speaker in Kannada and Hindi. And he wanted donations. And he sat with me for two hours. In those days I used to smoke the best cigarettes. No point in smoking cheap cigarettes. People may say, "Well, you get cancer in any case." So why not cheap cancer? Why not expensive cancer?

So he tried to persuade me that smoking is bad, this is bad, that is bad, everything is bad. I said, "What do you want?" He said, "I am a sanyasi. I am not supposed to ask."

I said, "If you don't ask, what shall I give you? Would you like one cigarette for instance?"

He said, "How can I smoke?"

"Will you have some coffee?"

"I don't think so."

"Will you have some tea?"

"No."

"Then what do you want?"

He said, "Some money. We need for the Mission."

I said, "What have you done in your sanyas?"

He said, "I have renounced even my mother."

I became so angry, because in Hindu shastra a mother is divine. She maybe anything but mother is divine. *Maatru devo bhava*, the Veda starts. The first thing is, *Maatru devo bhava*. Then *Pitru devo bhava*, then *acharya devo bhava*. Acharya comes only third. I said, "This is the situation in our Hindu culture and tradition and you have given up your mother. Aren't you stupid?" Even the great Adi Shankaracharya gave a promise to his mother that, "At the time of your death I shall come even though I have taken sanyas." He is a great example that sanyas does not absolve you of your duty to your parents, and one who takes refuge at the sanyas, to throw away his duties is a fraud. He is cheating the public. "No, no, I have no duties, sir!" His duties are more than our duties. We have only a duty to our families. Sanyasis have a duty to all society. A real sanyasi has a duty to the whole of the society in which he exists. Today they are parasites living on society, not stopping at any crime. Which is why Babuji said, "Ninety-nine point nine nine percent of our sanyasis are frauds." Don't go near a person who is yellow clad. There is also an ancient shastra that inside a house, a sanyasi and a *kachua* should never be allowed to enter. Both bring disaster with them!

So on one side we have a tradition of holiness, and our bowing before swamis, touching their feet.

You only have to wear yellow clothes and *ipso facto* they fall at your feet. They don't know what you are. So it is the clothes you are worshipping, not the man. On the opposite side you have a person like my Master who never adopted yellow clothes. He could walk the streets and nobody cared anything for him. They did not see the inner Reality.

Simplicity must come, whether in language or in existence or in designs of houses, by pruning away the complexity of structures and then bringing into our existence the essentiality behind it. Very much like Sahaj Marg is simple, not because it was like that, but because Babuji removed all the trash and the rubbish out of yogic systems. No *yama, niyama, asana, pranayama,* for instance. No *asan*; no sitting this way or that way. Pruning down to its simplest essential elements is simplicity. Now when we have a complex life and one by one we cut off, like pruning grapes in a vineyard—when the grapes are in harvest, if you have seen a farm like that, they cut away all things until only the bare things are left and they bring out new shoots and new branches, and you have a beautiful grape crop—pruning is what is necessary to bring simplicity. So let us not be confused by seeing these villagers wearing *langoties* and going in bullock carts and falling in dust and thinking they are simple. They are primitive. Please remember the difference between a primitive life and a simple life. Primitives are rarely simple in their material existence or even in their thinking way. They are extremely complex in their thoughts.

I remember once I went to my native village which I had never visited in Tanjore district. And I discovered the village with great difficulty, off the main road, and there was a man hammering nails on rafters and preparing for a house. I said, "Where is the *munsif* of that village, can you tell me. Where can I find him?" He said, "You go on this road three miles, then there is a temple. Just behind the temple is his house." So I found it. I located the house and said, "I have come to see the village *munsif.*" A lady came and said, "No, no, but he is there on the main road, hammering the beam and the rafters together. We are building a house. He is doing all the work himself." The man I had spoken to was the village *munsif* himself and that blighter sent me three miles away! Because in the meantime he wanted to think, "Why this man is coming here? Has he come to buy a house? Has he come to build a house? Does he want to buy land? How much money I can take from him?" Beware of villagers! In cities we are prepared for corruption, we are prepared to be robbed; we are safe. In villages, they are very simple, they are very nice, they are smiling at you all the time. Why I am saying this is not as a criticism against village life. It is a criticism against our misunderstanding of simplicity when it is only primitivity.

In music, it is a well known fact that a man must be a master at making the most complex creations of music, and then he comes over into simplicity. That simplicity is different from the simplicity which we thought was simplicity before he became a master of music. Like we have these fellows, street singers, you know, with *ektaras*, small instrument with one string, and they are able to play something on it. We say, "What beautiful, simple music," you see. An instrument costing four *annas*. But you buy it, you cannot play it. Nor can he play anything more than what he is playing all the time to sell his instruments. The true simplicity comes by mastering music in the most complex creations, complications; then comes the simplicity, like when you go over a mountain you come to the valley on the other side.

So following the Master must not be automatic, like ducks following each other, like cattle following each other, like sheep following each other, like politicians following each other. A leader in politics is there because he can offer something. And people go to him for what he can offer, not for his sake. The moment he falls from power he is left, in one mud hut somewhere without even a telephone sometimes.

So, please make sure you follow because you want to follow. You want to follow not because he can give you something but because you want **Him**. Then it becomes a legitimate act of bhakti, of love, without which it is all farcical. Otherwise, it is only like animals following each other, birds following each other. There is no love between birds when they fly in a flock. Two hundred thousand beautiful birds flying across the Pacific from Canada, the geese migrating. They love each other. Yes? Where is this love? Fish swimming in shoals—sometimes you can get two hundred and fifty tonnes of fish in one net. They don't love each other. It is an instinct. We call it the herding instinct. There is a word in English for it. Abhyasis should not fall a prey to this herding instinct. Abhyasis should seek to be with the Master because they love the Master, not even because you can get a transmission from him. Then it becomes something cheap, something commercial. He who wants nothing, gets everything; he who is nowhere, is everywhere; he who owns nothing possesses everything—see these are great concepts from our Indian tradition. And remember time has two faces. One in which we have to lose time, by prolonging time to fulfil our needs, which is mostly in the material sphere—that the more work you do, the more you earn; the longer you cook the better it is cooked, things like that. That bigger houses take longer to build than smaller houses, that the longer distance takes longer time—these are all material concepts of time. In the spiritual concept of time it comes from longer to shorter to almost timelessness. You must remember, I have written somewhere Babuji Maharaj said, "The greatest transmission is when we transmit from beyond time." And he said, "I have not yet found one person to whom I can give such a transmission."

So Masters are found not because of their inability to do things, but because they don't have the proper person on whom to do it. It is like having a pressure cooker in your house but nothing to cook at all. When you don't need to cook, what would you put in the pressure cooker?

So material existence grows into longer and longer periods of time. Spiritual existence comes into shorter and shorter periods of time. Ultimately he says, "Begin," and "That's all." And that is the greatest transmission. I am unfortunate because I had only a forty-five seconds transmission, but I think most of you are unfortunate because none of you got anything less than forty minutes or twenty-five minutes. So when are we going to develop in such a way that, as Babuji said, talking about his Master Lalaji, that with the blink of an eye he could grant liberation. He just looked like that and that's over. And Lalaji, when you presented some problem, he said, "*Achha!*" and it was over. It was not that there was some super-human power or some yogic *shakti* or *siddhi* that was used. It was his ability to contract time between cause and effect with almost zero time. Let us understand this very clearly. If I can just take a potato in my hand and by the time I give it to you it is baked, it is a super-human thing, it is a siddhi, it is a shakti, because potatoes cannot be baked without that much of heat. I may have had something in my hand which created the heat, but if you can make a sinner into a saint in one instant, it doesn't need any material medium for that transformation to take place.

There comes the question of spiritual authority, spiritual ability. I won't even use the word spiritual power because it is misleading. There is no power in Sahaj Marg. We don't use power here. There is forceless force, powerless power—all these concepts which Babuji Maharaj has repeated and we are repeating now, most of us without understanding these things.

So, I wish that we do not be misled by the superficialities of existence. I read somewhere recently, I think perhaps in the *Readers Digest,* they were talking of Peter the Great—that he was a great murderer, and the greatest pope was a rapist, things like that. Alexander the Great was another tyrant. We have this idea of greatness and big-ness in our society. He is a big man. Yes? In what sense? Nobility is a great concept, not because nobles were noble, but because they were called nobles, because they had nobility as character. Today we have nobles without nobility. Like we have coins without value. Inflation precisely means that our coins which were gold, then became silver, then it became copper, then it became nickel, and today if you blow it away, the rupee coin is flying in the air.

So conceptual understanding is very necessary, that a holy person need not be great. A great person need not be holy. A good person need be neither holy nor so great, nor simple. He is only good. We have got into this habit of mixing up all these ideas, that an actor, "Oh! What a lovely person." A cinema actor! Yes, lovely in what sense? That which can be loved is lovely. Loveable! By virtue of the necessity to express something, language develops. Now we are misusing language to corrupt our original concepts of what they should mean. It is an invertendo acting there. Like love today has become debased into lust. I have spoken about this so many times. Both four-letter words but with such enormous differences in concept and in meaning and in fundamental values. So, "I love him." What is the use of your loving him? You just want to go to bed with that guy. And just because somebody takes you to bed it means he loves you!

Half the tragedies—why half—ninety-five percent of the tragedies in the world today of broken hearts is because of this misunderstanding of what love is. In Hindu shastra it is clearly defined that *prema* is something, *kama* is something else. Prema is love. Kama is for the needs of procreation. You may or may not indulge in Kama. Therefore the idea of celibacy, the idea of withholding the usage of that enormously creative power to be used only for the moment of creation, not for fun, not for pleasure, not for destruction of the self or the other.

When we get back to the right understanding of these words, we will surely use words with greater effectiveness. Today half the misunderstanding created between people who speak together is because one person uses one word in one meaning and the other person understands it in a different meaning. Let us have an understanding. What is an understanding? Often it is money being passed under the table. *Samjotha ho gaya.* Several lakhs, sometimes crores, and it is called an 'understanding'. It is a misunderstanding of the word understanding! I would suggest that most of our modern problems emanate from misunderstandings of the basic concepts of simplicity, honesty, truth. In these three concepts, everything is there. If you know what is really simple, what is real honesty, what is truth, you would not have all these emblazoned *Satyameva jayate naanrutam*, and speak lies standing right under the Ashok pillar. Poor Ashok! And it is wrong understanding. As Babuji used to say, it does not matter if you tell lies to others, but don't tell lies to yourself. When we go on telling lies, it becomes a habit and we don't know when we are lying to ourselves even. It is like a man who produces drugs and medicines and who adulterates them, and they are killing society right and left, he doesn't care. One day his son falls sick and he buys the same drug and his son is dying with the same medicine that he has prepared for public use and which is now coming back to him in the form of nemesis. Anything let loose comes back. Not just yo-yos and boomerangs. Any thought let loose comes back. Emotions let loose come back. You weep, another person weeps and you start weeping because the other person is weeping, and it has one of these self-escalating effects.

So the saint has to be absolutely in control of himself, which means in all his functions, in all his faculties, all his emotions, his feelings, everything must be under his regulatory power. He cannot weep just because there is need to weep. He may be permitted to weep when there is perhaps no need to weep at all, but he understands the need to weep. Because by weeping he may be able to convert a thousand peoples' hearts into some simplicity and honesty. Essentially we must differentiate between living as we should and acting a farce life. Most of us are actors. "All the world is but a stage and men and women merely actors," Shakespeare said long ago. It was the truth then; it is the truth today. We play so many parts. I mean we are to be praised that we can play so many parts. We are not like actors who can only play Arjuna or only play Draupadi and nothing else. We are very versatile in our ability to play. But we have fallen a victim to that ability ourselves, imagining that I am Draupadi or imagining that I am such and such at that moment. We are deluding ourselves. Our play acting should not become self-delusionary mechanisms, which means that I and my personality must be two separate wings—I being in control of my personality, using it at will. Like Krishna could be so many things: he was a lover of the *gopis*, he was an adversary to his enemies, he was a friend to a friend, he was a bhakta to a bhakta, he could wash the feet of rishis. What did he not do in his lifetime? He could, precisely because he was everything. And who is everything? One who has mastered the self.

So a Master is not master of this or that. We can have masters of science, masters of medicine, masters of arts, but we don't have masters of spirituality. We only have Masters—precisely because they have not mastered anything outside, they have mastered everything inside. But when such a person who has mastered everything inside comes out, the whole of creation is like a ping pong ball in science, because what is inside is outside. What is outside is not inside. So this great secret, this great truth which has been known from times immortal in India but forgotten today is that, what you have inside, if you have regulated it, controlled it, mastered it, you are a Master of the Universe by virtue of that mastery. For you, time and space have no meaning. You can use space like a ping pong ball; you can use time as if it is a capsule. You can prolong a *yuga* into millions of years; you can contract it into a second. How could Krishna claim to have to known the Ikshvakus and Manu before that, and yet be talking to Arjuna on the battlefield? For him, time did not exist.

Often we confuse the ability to see back or see forward, *dirghadarshis*, as some ability to go beyond. It is not like that. He is able to telescope the two ends of the universe into one grand panorama right here. Like when you fly, you see enormous pieces of territory below you and they are all there at the same time. A car hundred miles away and a car hundred miles this side—you are seeing both. Because you are above; because you have gone beyond this dimension in which this is taking place into a third dimension from which you can see all of this dimension.

So spirituality essentially means, not acquisition of powers. It means transcending even powers, rising above. One who rises above powers, can use all powers. But if you have one power and you are a master of that power, that very power will kill you. This is also an ancient tradition, that he who lives by the sword shall die by the sword. If you extend it, he who lives by money shall die by money. Isn't it? So what is the difference?

Therefore spirituality, most especially Sahaj Marg, preaches, teaches and offers transcendence, not acquisition. Here we have to transcend everything, transcend existence itself. Transcend even, as somebody said, the need for a God. Why God? Because we are going before Him only as beggars. We have no intention of transcending. We are only subservient: "Please, God, give me this; please, God, save my child; please, God, give me a

193

promotion; please, God, let my lover come to me today!" And God laughs, you see. He says, "This damn fool, whom I have created in my image," which is a tradition that God created man in His own image. It is like the son going to the father and begging him. Putting on dirty clothes, rags, and singing *bhajans*: "*Pitaji hame do paisa de de.*" "*Aree, bewakoof!* Who are you? Have you forgotten who you are? You are my son! And you are coming to me for two paise? Everything you see is yours, not because you have earned it, not because you have acquired it but because you are my son." And here we all say we are children of the Master, and we go and beg before him. We are children of God, and we go and beg before Him, nauseatingly before Him, rolling in the ground before Him. If God ever destroys humanity, it will not be for its crimes and for its culpability and for its spite; it will be for its stupidity. That His children, we, have isolated ourselves to such an extent that we become paupers begging at the gate.

So let us beware of these ideas, that we have to beg of God, we have to pray to Him, we have to worship Him. Some of these travesties are today even propagated by Hinduism: Shiva is called *abhishekapriya*, and Vishnu *alankarapriya*. How can Vishnu be *alankarapriya* when his *alankara* is the whole universe? Does he need some more *alankara*? These are purely human concepts created by the priesthood for their continued existence. They can take what the poor man has to offer, and they can shave the rich man! "*Das hazar.*" "*Han han, koi baat nahin.*"

So you see, we have become so totally unfit to exist, not because God condemns us, not because destiny condemns us, but because we have isolated ourselves from that divinity which is our Father, which is our Creator, and today we are going before Him as supplicants, mendicants, beggars, begging for trivial things, which for Him don't exist at all. It is like children, you know, when you have a child and you take it to the beach and he is picking up pebbles, it is nice. He is a child. But if you take a twenty four-year old son with you to the beach and he is picking up pebbles and shells, we will go to the doctor. "What is this, doctor, you know, all his life he is has been doing this." And the doctor says, "What can I do, you know? He is mentally retarded, his mental age is three." So our spiritual age is zero. Had we been mature we could walk into the divine hall of the divine kingdom, and say, "Dad, come here!" And He will come. Only a son can call his father; nobody else can call. *"Pitaji"*—and you are awake—*"Beta kya baat hai."* Your friends cannot address you so freely; even your wife dare not. Though sometimes they may like to show their strength before the public, they make you run. But a son has that privilege, you see, because he is that *parampara* of creation. And in that what is the simplicity we are to acquire? Not simplicity in not shaving and growing your hair and having dirty clothes unwashed and admiring bullock carts and camels. This is not simplicity.

Simplicity means, reducing everything to the one, and when you are a divine *bhakta*, going only towards Him, it is no longer important what you are

195

wearing, how you are dressed, whether you bathe or not, whether you eat meat or not, avoid that or not. Because in your mind there is one and only one. It is the essential of existence, it is the most elemental existence which rules everything else. Such a person is a very simple person. I think I have said enough—breakfast will be ready—and we have to go again at eleven o'clock to brother's house, where all of you are invited, so please be ready.

Thank you.

Love

To understand love correctly is a very difficult task. I would like to say a few words in English, because this lady from France spoke of a disappointment, that there is no brotherhood. But I was giving the example of the solar system where the Sun is there and the planets are going round and round. If any planet made the mistake of thinking of any other planet, the whole solar system would collapse. But they are only looking towards the Sun which is the central source, which is holding everything together. Sometimes Venus and Mars are close together, sometimes they are far apart, what you call conjunction. It is not that when they are close they are friendly or together and when they are far apart they are enemies and there is no love between them. So nearness and farness have no meaning in love. The love and their oneness as a solar system, the parts of a system, is because they are all held together by the Sun, towards whom they are all looking, all the time. If they make the mistake of thinking they have to establish bonds of friendship, of affection, of love between the planets, that system will be destroyed. Everything will fall into the Sun and be burnt.

So love means a certain respectable distance between the lover and the beloved; love means not looking to anybody else for love; love means giving love, not hoping to receive love. So I would like to

Talk at Bahal on 26 April, 1990

emphasise this aspect to our Western brothers and sisters, because in the West love is an interpretation of receiving, not of giving; in the East it is solely devoted to giving, not to receiving at all. The truth of this matter being on that famous dictum that, "What you give shall come back to you multiplied many fold." So one who cannot give love can never receive love. There is no use in looking for it like a blind man searching in a jungle for a black cat. It will never happen. One who looks for love, to be loved, is doomed to despair, to frustration, to disappointment and ultimately to destruction. Because he is, or she is, working against the law of Nature, the fundamental law of existence, the divine law that, "Thou shalt give." I pray that all of you shall have this blessing of my Master that we shall learn how to give, to give fearlessly, to give generously, to give without even the idea that we are giving, which means to develop a self in which giving becomes the nature.

I have always wondered how the Sun would feel if it understood that every second it is burning millions of tonnes of fuel. It would perhaps say, "What is this, I am burning myself, destroying myself, let me not burn,"—and the Sun is dead. In burning itself is its existence. In burning, it sustains this part of the universe which we call our solar system. It provides us with light, with heat, with warmth, with agriculture, with the movement of the winds, of the tides. Everything that exists, to which we owe our existence, comes from that. Therefore in ancient India, and today, is the concept that the Sun is the ultimate which rules our being, our existence. And therefore this famous Gayathri mantra as a worship to the Sun. But as my Master clarified, it is for the power behind the Sun, not to the luminescent solar body. And the famous example of the humble candle is often used in the spiritual literature of this country, you see, that in burning itself, it gives light to others.

So you see, the spiritual life is not a life of getting and having, it is a life of giving and not having. My Master paraphrased it beautifully, when saying that a saint is not born to enjoy his life, but he is to be enjoyed by others. He gives. How can the giver of love, want love? It is crazy, you know! That I am the giver of love and I want love back. How can it happen? The giver of light does not look for light with which to give light. It is like a candle saying, "It is dark in that room, please illuminate it, then I shall go there." It would be stupid, it would be crazy, it would be against the nature of its existence. Can you imagine a candle asking for another to light the way into a dark room? It lights the way itself. It does not need any other light. Similarly the saint finds the love that he needs is in himself; therefore he can offer it to all. That which we do not have, we cannot give. That which we cannot give, we can never think of receiving.

So you see, the ancient law, which is still existing today, which shall always exist: "Give. In giving lies the plenitude of existence." This is your fundamental law of existence, this is your prime duty and sole duty. Learn to give, to give, and continue to give. And may Master bless you with this. Thank you.

Meditation and Education

Of course, you are all still children studying in schools and colleges. So, before we start answering your questions, I think I should tell you something about the role of meditation in preparing you for your education and for your future life. Generally, education should mean something which we have forgotten in this country. Nowadays education only means preparing yourself for a job, and people want to do something which will give them the maximum money for comfort, for good standard of living. But education really means to draw out of you your best in terms of your potentials, best in the physical way, i.e., to prepare you to be fit citizens who can serve society, serve your brothers and sisters, to draw out of you your mental and intellectual potential, not to cram facts into your heads. That is the unfortunate consequence of the material civilisation to which we have succumbed.

Really speaking, according to the Vedas, all knowledge is already in us. The only thing, it is covered by what they call ignorance, and they use the famous example of a mirror which is overlaid with dust. You clean away the dust and everything is clear. So, education is really the process of removing the ignorance that is covering our inner knowledge, which is absolute, which is perfect, which is eternal, which is supreme. We don't really have to learn anything. Very often people ask, "How

Talk at Jaipur on 28 April, 1990.

is it that saints and the great Masters of this world appear to know everything? You ask them any question, they have the answer." They are supposed to be the Masters of the past, the present, and the future. The Sanskrit word is *trikalajnani*. How is it possible? If you study the lives of all the ancients, the rishis, the saints, even up to Vivekananda, Ramakrishna Paramahamsa, few of them were really educated in the sense that they went to school. They had no degrees, but yet they were knowledgeable to the absolute extent that they knew everything. They could see. They did not learn and remember and speak. They could see as if everything is in front of them.

Now, this ability is created by meditation, because by meditation we learn to put our mind on one object. Meditation really means to think constantly, continuously of one subject. It has no other meaning. And whatever you think of, that is the object of your meditation, and all the ancient systems, modern systems of spirituality, of occultism all over the world, they say the same thing. "You will become that upon which you meditate." This is a old law: "As you meditate, so you become." That upon which you meditate, that you become.

Now when we are students, we are supposed to think continuously about our education. If this is done properly, naturally you become well-educated because your mind is going on that same thing, again and again and again. In spirituality, all that we do is to change the subject. Put divinity in place

201

of material life and when you meditate on God, you should become God. Anyway, that will come later.

But, as students, what concerns you all is, what has meditation to do with education *per se*. Now when we learn how to meditate properly by putting our mind on one object continuously, we become capable of concentration. So concentration is a result of meditation. There is an unfortunate misunderstanding, even in our yogic literature, that we have to concentrate. Concentrate on God. God is not an object. How can we concentrate on God? He has no physical form. He has no qualities. Therefore most people fail. Even the great aspirants, young fellows, students who have gone to jungle, they come back after ten years and say, "All a waste of time." Many people have been disillusioned by meditation, by these systems of yogic practice, not because the systems are wrong or incorrect, but because the way of doing it has been wrongly taught. They have been told to concentrate, when concentration is the end result of meditation.

So, when we learn to meditate and we meditate continuously, we use the mind itself to purify itself and to apply it on any chosen object. When we become capable of doing this by prolonged meditation—I don't mean by prolonged meditation, twenty-four hours at a stretch, but daily for a stipulated time—then on any object on which you put your mind its inner truth of its existence, of its being, is instantly revealed. Therefore the ancient and the modern gurus, the great avatars, the Purushas, the *Mahapurushas*, they have all said that, "Concentration is the instrument for revelation." So it is very easy, when you think of it that way, how these great seers, as we call them, the *drishtas*, how could they see, because they thought of something and they applied their mind to it totally and everything about it was revealed. Even whether it is in the future or the past, it did not matter. So, when you look at a person, everything about that person is revealed. When they look at an object, everything is revealed. Now, in this way, if you are able to spare, say half an hour in the morning, half an hour in the evening for the practice, for the system of meditation, you are really training your mind to be able to meditate, then subsequently to concentrate to become a capable instrument for revelation. Can you realise the enormity of the benefit that you will get, when your mind is so trained, that instantly you apply it? You take a history book, and you open it, and everything you read is instantly revealed. You don't have to memorise. When was Akbar born? When did the Mughal dynasty came to an end? All this is only cramming facts. It is said that Swami Vivekananda, one of our greatest personalities, would put a book under his pillow and go to sleep. He did not even open it, and in the morning he knew everything about the book. If you ask him what is on page 216 in paragraph two, he could recite the whole paragraph, not because he opened it and memorised it but because his mind applied, photographed, and everything was stored here, like a computer stores information.

So, what is the relevance of meditation? This is the relevance of meditation. Now we are struggling with our merely human minds—some of which is stupid, some of which is very sensible, something is under our control, something is rebelling. You know, as students, sometimes you are not able to study, you sit down on the table with your book open with all your best intentions, but you are not able to study, or a friend comes and calls you and you are not able to resist the call of the friend, or your mother switches on the television and that is pulling you there, or you smell something, *chaat masala,* and there goes your thought into the kitchen. All not because they are tempting us but because our mind is not in our control.

Meditation trains us to become the master of our minds. It must obey what I say; not I obey my mind. That is why most children, most youths, especially between the age of say twelve and eighteen, nineteen, twenty—very troublesome age. Some of you must have experienced the problem of 'growing up', as we say, because you have no control over your mind. It is being buffeted about like leaves in the wind. Then you say, "Mummy, I can't help it, what can I do?" and sometimes you weep, sometimes you go to your father. If you are a daughter, he is very nice. If you are a son, he may give you a couple of nice affectionate taps on your head, but what is the result? Loving will not produce education. Education must be produced only by application: application of the mind, and the mind must be able to concentrate, and that concentration can only be developed by meditation. There is no second way.

So, this is the relevance of meditation through the educational process. I would go to the extent of saying that without meditation your educational process is incomplete. It is like building a house without a foundation. Therefore you find today misfits in every sphere of life: so-called educated people who don't know their subject; engineering graduates who construct a bridge which is collapsing even before it is completed; houses not even in vertical, rooms badly designed, switches not accessible, electrical circuits faulty. They are educated people but they are not able to apply their education. You have to learn to apply the mind to become educated, you have to learn to apply education to use education, like the difference between science and technology. Science is pure, technology is application of that science to producing things, to utilising things.

Now, how is all this possible? I would stress this point, that without meditation your whole educational edifice is built on something like sand. Therefore, we have degrees but no knowledge. Today our country, I am unfortunately compelled to say this, is full of degree holders, even PhDs in science and mathematics, and this, that, and the other, who know exactly what they have studied from their books and nothing more, because they have studied only what they had to study to get their degree. Passing has become our main consideration, not education; and passing—not just passing, but if possible with a good rank, so that we can study higher, become a doctor, become an engineer. Why? We can make a lot of money.

So to keep our educational system pure, education must mean education and nothing else. Like food, the moment you put colour in it and this, that in it, that food is useless. Food must be simple, tasty, nourishing. Why should it be colourful and beautiful to look at? So, we have made our educational process something like a commercial enterprise. Now, when we go back to meditation, there are two benefits. One, as I said, we train the mind to be able to apply itself on any object that you choose and therefore revelation becomes available to you, which means in an instant total grasp of the subject, not page by page, paragraph by paragraph, chapter by chapter, not at all. It becomes a total thing, like when you illuminate a place, everything you see before you is illuminated. It is not illuminated piecemeal. You may see it piecemeal, but the whole thing is illuminated. When the sun rises in the morning, everything is illuminated at once.

So, meditation gives this power of instant and total illumination to the mind on anything that it may be applied. Secondly, because it is a process of training yourself to master yourself, I would suggest that material ambitions, sort of take second place. They don't become the primary object of your existence or your education, but they take second place. And you get the confidence that if I can master myself, I can master anything else. If I am educated in the real sense, not just with facts but with knowledge of a subject, I must be able to do the work that anybody gives to me. If I do the work in the right way, it is done in the right way, it must be fruitful. If it is fruitful, the work itself is my reward. Not the money that I am going to earn. After all, today even barber shops flourish; *panwalahs* flourish. I am told there are panwalahs who make a thousand rupees a day and, as the businessman of our country say, they don't even pay tax—thirty thousand rupees a month without paying income tax. But they are not educated, they are stupid. They may build houses but they are stupid. Their toilets and their bathrooms are dirty. Their staircases are filthy, because they are spitting everywhere. Education must give us culture. Education gives culture because we look to the inner values of things, not to the superficial dresses and *tikas* that we put on our shoulders and our foreheads.

So, meditation confers on us a total integrated blessing by making us educated in the true inner sense, educated to values and not to facts, educated to our inner needs, not to apparently social needs, that I must be better than my peers, I must earn more money than my younger brother, not things like that, but to the true values of existence. In this way, meditation is the foundation not merely for education but for our existence.

So having said this, now I am sure you have questions to ask. I am prepared to answer whatever I can, you will excuse me, if I have no answer for some questions.

Thank you.

Q: Generally meditation is something linked with the people who practice in older age. How can it help us achieve at our age?

A: You have just heard my talk. I have clearly stated that it is the foundation for education itself. So obviously it must begin when we are young. Now unfortunately in our country, there is this funny idea that human beings should get on with their living, have their fun, exhaust themselves physically, mentally, morally, and then when they have nothing else to do, then come to meditation. God is generally the subject of our desperate need, not of our love. Even though in India we always say, God is love. But we think when nothing else is available, then we should go to God, therefore old people go to God. But generally what the great Masters have said is, "If you come to meditation when you are too old, then you have no longer the ability to control or regulate your mind. It's like an old man of ninety-two wanting to walk. He cannot walk.

So everything that is worth doing is worth doing when we are young, including meditation. Actually, according to the ancient Indian system of shastras and our spiritual way of life, the initiatory process must start at what they call *garbhaashtaka*, that means the eighth year from the day of conception; that is assuming one year passes in your mother's womb, when you are seven, initiation must be given, and from that time your meditation and spiritual life must begin. But as I said, material life has taken over, and they say, "+No, no, let us make our money. Let us build our houses. Let us have our *tamasha*." And then when we are too old for everything else, then we take up meditation, which is wrong.

Q: I am thinking of a career in sport. I would like to know how meditation will help?

A: Have you heard of Arjuna? A great warrior. Nowadays you are seeing the Mahabharata, everybody is familiar. It is said that when Draupadi's *swayamwara* was to take place, these Pandavas went in the guise of Brahmins. All the *shishyas* of Drona were there, the great archers, but it was Arjuna who not only won the archery contest but won Draupadi for the Pandava brothers, too. Because, through spiritual practice, he was a disciple of Lord Krishna. As you know, he was a friend of Lord Krishna and a disciple of Lord Krishna. And through the spiritual training under the Master Drona, who was not merely a master of archery, he was a Guru, an *acharya*, you see. They were taught to meditate, to concentrate, aim and fire.

So this test had this wheel, and a parrot on top of it, and the wheel was rotating, and there was a pond below and you had to look into the pond, look at the reflection and shoot. And when Arjuna was victorious, Drona asked each one, "Why did you fail and what happened?" One said, "I saw the wheel," another said, "I saw the space through the spokes," third one said, "I saw the parrot," but Arjuna said, "I saw the eye of the parrot reflected in the pool and I shot."

So, you see, if you can be a successful warrior and an archer, why can't you be a successful sportsman? Because after all, in sports, there are two things that are necessary. Sportsmanship, and the ability to concentrate on what you are doing. Sportsmanship is an attitude of the heart, that in sports, there is both victory and loss. And the famous dictum, that we play not to win but for the sake of the game. This generosity or the acceptance, the humility to accept that failure is an ever-present possibility, and therefore we play only for the game, not to be victorious. And victory goes to the one who can concentrate. Both these abilities are developed by meditation.

Anybody else? Yes please?

Q: We are confused about our career in future. How can it help us in that?

A: The future is evolving out of the past, isn't it? Tomorrow cannot come without today. If today suddenly this world should be destroyed, God forbid, there won't be any tomorrow. So the foundation for tomorrow is today. But we must go one step backwards and realise that the foundation for today existed yesterday. So in what I did yesterday lies the success or the fruitfulness of today's life. And in what I shall do today lies the future. Justification for my existence, the fruitfulness of my living. So today's existence is what really matters in thinking of the future. Now most students are only thinking of the future and forgetting the today. Therefore they don't study today, they don't meditate today, they don't play today. Three things are very necessary. My Master, my Guruji used to tell me, "We should play as if we are working, and we should work as if we are playing." You know, there is another statement from another famous philosopher, who says, "Drink solids and eat liquids." That is, there should be an opposition, or a tendency to look at things from an opposite perspective. If you are too serious about serious things, as the English proverb goes, you may miss the wood for the trees. So, if you do correctly what you are to do correctly, the future is already taken care of. And to do correctly what you have to do correctly, you must be able to control your mind, regulate your mind, make it an instrument capable of revelation. And this we achieve through meditation. So, this is the relevance of meditation, even to the future and even to your career. Thank you.

Yes?

Q: Sir, I am trying to learn meditation by reading books.

A: You are trying to learn meditation by reading books? Well yes, because nowadays the world is full of books which are trying to teach you how to do things. This is putting the cart before the horse, as we say. Can you learn to swim by reading a book? Can you learn to cook by reading a book? You can read a book but you have to side by side cook also. Similarly, here you are allowed to read a book but side by side meditate also. Now you cannot do both things at once. See, most of the ladies or girls who have tried to cook with a book in their hands have either burnt their fingers or burnt the thing that they are cooking or burnt the book also! So you read

211

first, then you cook. Taste it, if it is wrong, see what mistake you made, refer to the book. Then start all over again. And when you are perfect, you close the book and put it away. So the book is only to help you to begin something, not to complete something.

So similarly, books on meditation can tell you what meditation is. For instance, when I speak to you, you can think of me as a "speaking book." You don't have to turn the pages; I am doing it for you! Isn't it? I don't say "Page one, page two, page three, paragraph one..." like that. I tell you meditation is the ability to think of something continuously. Do it, sit down, close your eyes and try to think of one thing continuously. See if you are able to do it. If you are able to do it, you have already started meditation.

So the need for books is only to introduce us to do something, but most people, I find, have libraries—how to be a good carpenter, how to be a good musician, how to repair electrical appliances—they are never even opened. So yoga says, "Learn by doing. Because by doing you have taken the first step which is necessary: that is, to start doing something. It's like walking. If I am sitting in my chair and thinking of walking and reading books on how to walk well, at what rate I should walk, what should be my pulse rate, then I can never walk. I am sitting in my chair. Half an hour is gone. But if I get out and start walking the process is already begun. So it is better to do things and learn things because you are gaining two things by doing: you are learning how to do it; and you are getting the experience of doing. In books perhaps you only learn how to do things without ever doing it, therefore when you start doing it, you feel. Right?

Next? Yes, please.

Q: I want to learn more about concentration.

A: Concentration? Ah! What is there to know more? What is there to know more? Concentration is—for instance, we prepare coffee, we have the powder and we pour boiling water over it and all the essence is taken out of it, which you call the decoction. The rest is rubbish, you throw it away, like saw-dust.

Concentration in one sense is the ability to take the essence of anything which you wish to know. Now, you are a human being. You go to a Master, a spiritual Master. He doesn't want to know your height and the colour of your eyes, and how beautifully you can smile. Your passport needs these things. When you apply for a passport, they need your age, date of birth, parentage, all these things, colour of the hair, distinguishing marks. But for the saint it is your inner essence that he wants. Now this inner essence cannot be known by looking at the outer characteristics. They may be beautiful, they may be ugly, it doesn't matter. You cannot know bread by looking at breads; you have to eat it. So to know the essence of physical things, human beings and of the cosmic phenomena, the moment you are able to concentrate—now you know when you have a torch light and you concentrate by focussing it, the beam is powerful, it reveals everything within that beam. And I told you in the beginning, everything is revealed. It doesn't reveal only the good things and not the bad things.

213

So when we want to learn to concentrate, we must be prepared to meditate first. Secondly we must be prepared to have the faith and the courage to see what is shown to us, not to be disturbed by it. Not to be attracted by the beauty that we see, not to be repelled by the ugliness that we may see. When you look at a human heart, there may be so many things in it. Now suppose you say, "Oh, what a dirty person! No, no, I don't want..." you are no longer worthy to be called a person who can concentrate.

So concentration means the instant ability to draw the essence of anything upon which you apply your mind. Right?

Next please.

Q: I know something about meditation, but we don't have time. What to do?

A: Time. Unfortunately, there is an old saying that anything in this world can be recreated but not time. You can lose health, you can recreate it; you can lose money, you can make it again. Isn't it? You can burn a book, you can write it again. You can spoil the cooking that you are doing but you can make it all over again. But time passed is time lost. Once we understand this, that inevitably, inexorably time is limited to twenty-four hours a day, the second step comes: then we will understand how to use that time. Isn't it? After all, we cannot create two hours more. Then we will have what we call time consciousness and the ability to guide our life by this concept that time is limited, therefore the most important thing must be done first, the second important thing second, the not important thing not at all.

Now when people say they have no time, it only means they are doing useless things and not doing the things that they have to do. I have found that people who say they have no time are not doing anything at all, because there is another famous statement, "He who is most busy has the most time." For instance, one man, a senior government officer came to my Master. He also said the same thing that you are saying. You are saying it as a child, he said it as an old man.

He said, "But I have no time."

So my Guruji replied, "It is unfortunate that God created only a day of twenty-four hours. It would have been nicer if he had done it with twenty-six hours."

Then he laughed and said, "Even then you would have had no time, because you are not really interested in meditation." Then another man came. Same question. So my Master said, "Can you think of somebody more busy than you are?"

He said, "What! What a silly question. There are millions of people who are more busy than me."

Babuji said, "No, no. Tell me one instance."

He said, "The Prime minister of this country is very busy."

Babuji said, "How much more busy?"

He said, "Enormously more busy."

Babuji said, "If he can find all the time to do all that he is doing, being enormously busier than you, how is it you don't find enough time to meditate for half an hour?"

So, time—I have also found this in my own experience—the more you do, the more time you seem to have. Because time is utilisation. As one man used to tell me, an hour has sixty minutes, and it has three thousand six hundred seconds. And if you can do one thing in each second, you can do three thousand six hundred things in an hour. Imagine how much you can do in twenty-four hours. But we are wasting our time, looking out of the window with the history book open before us. Suddenly you wake up and find it is two and a half hours gone in daydreaming. And you say, "I have no time, mummy, what can I do? Tomorrow is my test," and you go and weep. What is the use?

We have enough time. We have more time than we need. The secret is to apportion the time to what we have to do.

Next question, if any? Yes please?

Q: Can meditation help a drug addict?

A: Can meditation help a drug addict? Well, if you mean can it help you to become a better addict, no! We don't want better addicts. But, meditation can help, only after you have given up the drugs. You see, for meditation, as I said in the beginning, you are using the mind to train itself. And if the mind is not in your control, you cannot meditate. So the first thing for drug addict is to give up drugs. You know, it is like cycling. When you are cycling, if you have

216

to walk you have to get off the bicycle. You cannot walk and bicycle at the same time. Now the most dangerous thing about drug addiction is it destroys the brain cells. After a particular stage, especially if you are on the heavy stuff like LSD and what not, the brain cells are damaged irreversibly. And then you become incapable of meditation. I won't say unfit because nobody is unfit. But if the brain cells are destroyed beyond the capacity that you can control yourself, use the mind itself to train it, it cannot help any more.

So people who want to help themselves must do it when they are capable of helping themselves. And drugs in this case are a very very dangerous thing and a very destructive thing. So drugs must be given up first. Once it is given up and you have the natural ability over the mind that any human being has, then you start the process of meditation, you will find everything that is unnecessary is thrown off. Now normally in yogic practice there is a lot of talk about renunciation and *vairagya* and all these things which frightens us. "Oh, how can I give up..." so many things, you see, money, power, girl-friends. Today's life is full of these things. But, what is necessary to life? You know, if you are going to fly, you are allowed only twenty kilograms baggage. Why? Because the plane cannot fly with unlimited weight. And then we find we don't really need twenty kilos. We need eight kilos of baggage and you have enough for a world voyage. So when we are limited by essentials, essential concepts of existence, then we are able to prune away all the unnecessary things. That is itself going towards a revitalisation of existence, by seeking to home in to the essence, forgetting the fripperies and the flapperies. Today in life everything is frippery and flappery. You want to buy a suitcase, there is more of ornamentation than suitcase in it; there is more of price. They are praising the handles and the bolts and nuts, but what about the suitcase itself?

So drugs are taking you to an illusory world. People talk of the reality that is, you know, a drug reality. I am ashamed to see that even great psychologists have talked of the alternate universe of drugs. Nonsense, I say. How can illusion be a reality? If you understand that illusion can never be a reality, then an illusory world can never be a real world. But children have been damaged by being taught wrong things. By saying there is a spiritual value even in illusion, which is like saying dreams are reality. So if I sit down and dream that I am a rich man, in some way there is a reality to my dream? It's crazy!

So, meditation can help only if the drug habit is given up, then by the natural process of evolution you are able to attain the perfection that you are looking for.

Next? Yes please.

Q: I feel nervous before exams. How to overcome it?

A: Nervousness is caused by two things. A state of un-preparedness and the consequent fear. If I have to fight you, and you are armed and I am not armed, naturally I am frightened.

Master at Sanchi

Master addressing the abhyasis at Mumbai

So, it follows that if you are prepared, you are not going to be nervous. No preparation—one young lady asked the question of time. If you have used your time properly, and given importance to the important things, automatically you are going to be better prepared than anybody else, better prepared than even your examiners, because you are fully prepared, they are only prepared with a few questions. You see, if a student studies well with full application of the mind, he can go beyond his teachers. The whole secret of yoga is that a real student of a real master must go one step ahead of his guru. And it is said that all the gurus from the most ancient times have wept their hearts at not being able to find one student like that. After all, the teacher is only looking through various chapters and trying to find something to ask you. But if you know your subject, you can ask that fellow some question which he will not be able to answer.

I remember once I had to go for an interview and there they asked me several questions. And one question I could not answer. So the man in the interview board said, "My friend, you have not been able to answer this question." I said, "Sir, you are all great people, on an interview board. If I ask you one question from your matriculation curriculum will you be able to answer?" He smiled, but that smile was answer enough! Reverting to what I said in the beginning, they are educating themselves only to attain a position. Having attained the position, the facts are forgotten, because they were never really educated. They only mastered the facts.

So if your aim is to educate yourself, not just to master some facts to answer questions, there will be never any fear. Because, now you have only mugged up something. Your main fear is that these questions should come which you have prepared for and not something else! Isn't it? So, if you are meditating, then going back to this rigmarole, and your mind had been prepared and everything has been revealed to you, there can be never any fear. Therefore it is said, meditation produces fearless people.

Next?

Q: Is it possible to get rid of some bad habits like...

A: Yes, you see, I have often thought about temptations. This is a question of temptation. You have your books on one side and the cinema on the other side and you go to the cinema. People say, "He was tempted by the pictures. He was tempted by his friends. He was tempted by drugs. He was tempted by... so many things." I have often thought, "What is really temptation?" Now, if a picture is a temptation, anybody who goes to that must be tempted. So the temptation is not in the object. It is in your response to the object.

Now yogic science says, yogic psychology says, we have a set of samskaras within ourselves, which are impressions created by our past thoughts and past actions. And when these are repeated, the impression becomes stronger and stronger. So the more pictures you see, the more of pictures you will tend to see. It is like the famous law of Newton, that anything going in a particular direction will continue in that direction until it is stopped. Any object in motion will continue to be in motion until stopped by another force. So to stop you from seeing pictures, another opposing force must have to stop you. Now an opposing force does not mean your parents or your friends or your teachers. It can be yourself, because yogic science says, "In me there are two selves: my outer superficial ego self and my inner eternal atomic self which is an *amsha* of the Divine." That must stop me from doing it. Now to enable that to stop me, I must give predominance to that which is in me which I call the Self. Therefore when we meditate, we are subduing this outer self, sitting quietly, calmly, in repose, and allowing the inner self to develop to its peak. Now when I begin to listen to the voice of my inner self, which we normally call conscience, and now, in control of myself, there is no external authority to say, "Thou shall not do this; Thou shall do this. Thou shall have no girl-friends. Thou shall have no addiction to drugs. Thou shall not smoke." It is so nonsensical to be told, "Thou shall not, Thou shall not, Thou shall not," for everything. But when you yourself tell yourself from your inner self, you just smile and say, "What is so wonderful about a picture? I will study today and better myself." So in that sense meditation will help you to conquer everything, not only pictures. Everything, totally, in the external universe.

Are there any more questions? I hope this is the last.

Archives

Brothers and Sisters

We have had some books released today, in different languages. For the sake of information I would like to tell you today that we have a complete set of Babuji's works. In fact, some of them have run into more than one edition. Superbly printed, superbly bound, they are sold extensively in France and in Switzerland and in other French-speaking countries. Apart from that we have some German translation, we have one or two in Dutch, we have one in Danish, and so it goes on. You will also be pleased to learn that *My Master* has been translated in Russian, because we have a centre in Russia now, in Minsk. It is not published as a book yet, but it is available as a translation, and it is being computer printed for distribution to abhyasis. The latest addition is the Japanese translation of the *Practice of Sahaj Marg*. I am happy to say that we have the first Japanese preceptor, I don't know if she is here, Michiko-san. She has done excellent work, and so we have the first possibility of the eastern wing of the Mission being developed. She is here before you.

So, I would say, in India of course, you all know we have translations in Telugu, in Kannada, in Tamil, in Marathi, in Gujarati, in Hindi of course. And one remark I would make is the problem of sales is as troublesome today as it was when Babuji Maharaj made that remark. We have had to suspend production because we are not even able to sell even five hundred copies. So the situation, I can say, is sound only in respect of English publications, where we produce three thousand copies of each work and we are able to sell them within two years generally. For language translations, it takes a much longer time in India.

Our books are very valuable. We have of course *Constant Remembrance*, which is a magazine published in America. Many of you are subscribers to it. It's a quarterly. We have a Danish magazine by the same name, *Constant Remembrance*. Now we have one published from Switzerland, which is called, I think, *Sahaj Marg Magazine* which has two languages, French and German. So the work goes on, you see. And so far we have restricted these to Babuji's works and some of the other authoritarian works of the Mission. For the first time we have this anecdotal publication, *Tears and Laughter*, which you will all read today, I hope. It has some very moving experiences, relating Babuji's and some of the abhyasis' interactions, how they felt, what happened. Some are very short, some are little longer, but all have their own emotional impact when we read them. Now I will here inform you that I am very grateful to our American and Canadian brothers of our North American Publication Committee who are computerising all the publications, preparing them for publication and printing them in the States, Tom Whitlam does most of the work in Canada and printing is done in the

US, the biggest benefit being that I receive the duplicate copies of the photographic negatives and straightaway print off everything here, without having the problem of composing and proof-reading, and all that. It is an enormous saving of labour for us and in a sense it is a transfer of technology, and in a sense also it is a cost saving for us, because as anybody concerned with publication industry knows, composing and printing take up a large slice of the total work. So I am beholden to them for that itself and it will continue in the future, too. *Tears and Laughter* also was published in the States first, and we have followed very quickly with the first Indian edition, which is an exact duplicate in every way and far cheaper, because the American edition is sold at ten dollars a copy, we are here selling it at fifty rupees a copy. The difference is substantial, largely because we are saved all the trouble in composing, proof-reading.

Now I have to make some request, you see. I think brother Kamalesh Patel remarked that some of the abhyasis have not been included there for lack of space. It is our intention that there are several volumes of *Tears and Laughter*—the one that has been released today is the first volume. To preserve a certain integrity and flavour, and emotional response to Babuji, it was my intention to restrict the first volume to only Western abhyasis. Similarly, we shall restrict to Indian abhyasis subsequent volumes. I hope eventually, there will be twenty-five volumes, fifty volumes. But it depends on your response to the request that I now make. If there is a wealth of material of people's interaction with

Babuji Maharaj, it is in India, where people have been associated with him from 1945 or even earlier. I would welcome contributions in English or Hindi first, so that we can have our edition of *Tears and Laughter*, which the West will duplicate for their circulation. Please take this request seriously, don't be shy about revealing the soul, because when you have to reveal your inner and deeper connection of love with your Master, you have to bare yourself, you have to bare your heart, you have to bare your soul. Otherwise there is no *Tears and Laughter*.

People have just watched what happened on the screen after Abhimanyu died, and how many people there were having wet eyes there we could see. There must be pathos, there must be bathos, there must be humour. Life is a mixture of all these things. There must be happiness of meetings, sorrow of parting, there must be the sorrow of not having fulfilled our goal, yet there must be the happiness of recording Babuji's praise, the chagrin of recording sometimes his criticism, recording his sorrow, his joy, matched by our own reactions about moments, sometimes a tenderness, sometimes a weakness, sometimes a highly charged emotional situation.

What I am trying to suggest is, unless we are very frank and very open, if we release these things, and I know it is like asking a lover to publish his beloved's love letters, they are very sacred, they contain the sweetness and the sourness of life blended into it. Written in the long path of yesterdays and day before yesterdays, but if they have relevance to the todays and tomorrows, it is our duty to reveal all these things for posterity, starting as of now. So it's no use just reading other people's reactions to their interactions with Babuji Maharaj. We have to contribute our own little bit. I am sure that there is nobody here who has not something to contribute. As I said initially, we will restrict it to English and Hindi, as I told you, for want of proper markets in other languages, but they will follow. Perhaps the translation, perhaps the original. This is a sincere request. I hope all of you will oblige by sending to me personally your contributions. There will be nothing confidential about it because they are going to be published.

So please make sure that you send it direct to me. It is only for purpose of correction and edition. There will be no rejections, but there will be a certain collection based on a particular tenor in a particular publication. That job the editors will do.

I have also to tell you now that we are starting publishing letters of Babuji Maharaj written to various abhyasis. And we commence with Babuji's letters to Dr. K. C. Varadachari. I think it will run into one set of three volumes and I hope to have the pleasure of requesting Brother Sarnadji to release it later this year, perhaps in July or August or September sometime. It is being prepared for publication. I hope to release it as a set of three or four volumes. Inevitably the price will be a bit high, but inevitably you will reap the benefits of all that correspondence that Babuji Maharaj had to do in the initial stages. There is enormous benefit in reading the letters again and again. Because there are so many clarifications there. So much wisdom is packed into those letters. So much of his love shines from those letters that I would be compelled to say anybody is foolish if they don't acquire them to read.

I hope to follow it with subsequent sets, one set per year. Unfortunately we have not been able to get some correspondence from certain sources in this connection, I will also say that for the last two or three years I have been making public requests that anybody who has Babuji's letters in the original may kindly hand them over to me and I will provide Xerox copies for you. But inevitably some people consider it too sacred a thing. I don't know what they will do, keeping in their homes, for there it will have a limited life. You all know the tragic story of how Lalaji's writings were sold away as waste paper by a maid servant in the house. It is my sincere hope and prayer that this should not be the state of Babuji's correspondence. All right thinking, right intentioned people will surely heed my request and respond by submitting to me. They will not be returned as they will form part of the archives of the Mission. I hope all of you will respond even if it is only one post card. But I need the originals. You will have to duplicate in the form of Xerox copy. The contents are always with you. And like situations, the personal memory is always yours. When you read *Tears and Laughter*, you may respond emotionally because there is a certain resonance from your heart to the heart of the situation that is written there. But the original is always the one who participated. Ours is only a vicarious relationship. I think that will be a big undertaking for us, because eventually I hope we shall have at least thirty to forty volumes of Babuji Maharaj's letters to abhyasis all over the world. In most cases unfortunately, I have only Babuji's letters to the abhyasi concerned. We don't have copies of the reply or the original letters written by the abhyasis themselves to Babuji Maharaj. It would have been a very complete thing if we could have had the total exchange of correspondence published. But in many cases it is not possible, for which I regret.

So this year will see, I hope, the release of the first set of the letters of Babuji Maharaj. The first has been restricted to his correspondence with Dr. K. C. Varadachari, one-sided, in the sense that they are only letters of Babuji Maharaj to Dr. Varadachari, the return letters are not available for publication, so I hope all of you start saving some money for it, because three volumes inevitably means a hundred to hundred and fifty rupees. They will be well bound, printed on good paper, worth preserving. I may also say here, that the only way of preserving these sacred things is to copy and distribute as widely as you can. Because inevitably destruction occurs. Through loss, through fire perhaps, through carelessness, through children tearing them up, maid-servants selling them off, termites—the way of destruction is multi-fold. But when we have thousand, two thousand, five thousand copies spread out throughout the world, somewhere they will always be available. So in that sense we are hoping to preserve these spiritual documents of the Master. Hopefully within our lifetime to the next and to the third generation after that.

I seek all your co-operation, and in your co-operation will continue the activities of the Mission, because the Mission is nothing but all of you put together. Like a state is made up of its citizens— *Bharat sabse mahan,* only when the people are *mahan*! There is no use trumpeting this from housetops! *Sara jahan se achha Hindustan hamara,* only when the people are *sabse achha. Desh* has no entity, it has no character, it is what the people of the country make of it. In the same way, the Mission will be what you all make of it, and what you are able to hand down as a sacred trust to the generation that will follow.

So please bear in mind that these requests are not only for us, it is for the Mission, it is for the archives of the Mission to be held in trust for the future. I pray for Babuji's blessings for all of you.

Thank you.

Message

Respected Elders,

We are assembled here in Jaipur to celebrate the Birth Anniversary of our Beloved and Revered Master, Param Pujya Babuji Maharaj. May this auspicious occasion confer his blessings, and his love and mercy, upon all his sincere devotees.

Recently a thought has been coming to me, off and on, again and again, and it is a refrain from an old song from the Tamil version of the film on Meera Bai, where Meera sings about Lord Krishna, saying, "Oh, my heart! Oh, my heart!" I refer to this because there are two ways of looking at the divinity that is our Master: one as the Master who is outside, an adorable person, an all-powerful person, and a fine person, beautiful, handsome and everything else. But the other way, and the mystical or the spiritual way, is to think of Him as our heart itself. I would suggest that we should not even think of Him as residing in our heart, but as **being** our heart itself. Then we will understand that, as we look after the physical organisation which is our body, within which the heart is the most important, the health of the heart is the most important, and the flow of vital oxygen-bearing blood from inside out, and again into the heart is the most important, and therefore the heart care has become the most important thing in the modern life. Similarly, in spiritual practice, we

---

Talk at Jaipur on 30 April, 1990.

should think that our spiritual heart, which is our Master, is the Ultimate person seated in us, functioning as our heart, and we should look after it with at least as much care and responsibility as we look after our physical hearts.

If you are able to do this, you will find that everything that you do that is good, productive and evolutionary is helping the heart to grow stronger and stronger, bigger and bigger, expanding outwards into the Universe, ultimately engulfing the Universe itself within itself. Whereas everything that one does against nature, which means that, without thinking of moral and immoral, good and bad, all these opposites of existence, anything that we do against nature becomes restrictive of this heart, makes it more and more solid, makes it enclosed, and eventually the heart may stop beating altogether. Of course I refer to both the spiritual and the physical hearts. It is more disastrous for the spiritual heart to stop beating than material heart to stop beating. The stoppage of the material heart, after all only puts an end to this life, but it is the spiritual heart that must go on beating its pulse right through the eternity that is the vastness, the immensity of our existence, so that we merge into that infinite Being, the ultimate Being, so that we can partake of its infinity, of its ultimacy.

Therefore in our spiritual life we should think of the Master himself as the heart, not just as someone who is seated in the heart, or as illuminating the heart from inside. Though in the beginning this practice is given to us by my Master, that He is there, the divine is there, and because of

His presence, divine illumination, divine light is illuminating the heart from inside. I am proposing this thought, that He is the heart also. Like we say, when somebody lives in a house, he is there. If it is Dr. Lalita's house, it is because Dr. Lalita lives there. If somebody else lives there it is not his house. So the heart becomes divine not by being divinised by some external agency, but because the divine itself is there. And where God is, that becomes the temple, and the temple is no longer something of a temporary nature, though it may be constructed of bricks and stones. Nevertheless, at least in our *samskriti*, in our dharma, we call it eternal, because the abode of the Ultimate cannot be tampered with.

I think this is the next stage in our spiritual belief, in our spiritual conviction. And in this way we should look upon the Master not as someone external to ourselves, not even as someone internal to ourselves, but as our very Self. I pray that by the Master's grace this sort of development may be blessed upon all of us so that we feel that the Master is there as part of ourselves, not as one separate from us, who is to be invoked again and again, who is to be looked to for advice and assistance, who is to be looked to for support, but as our very self within, and therefore part of ourselves, remembering that in this context, anything that happens to us is from our own self.

I think this is a very beneficial way of looking at the Master because then we have no external authority outside ourselves, or even inside ourselves, who is rewarding us or punishing us, but the onus for the whole performance of our existence, for the conduct of our life, becomes Self-oriented, and we become responsible to ourselves for everything that happens to us, for everything that we do, even for our spiritual evolution to the highest.

I pray that Master may bless us with success in this endeavour. I think this is an important aspect, because I find that even now we are praying to Master as somebody else, separate from us. The whole idea of prayer, I had once to discuss with Babuji Maharaj, and I suggested to him that prayer may even be considered as some sort of impertinence. Because we are seeking to remind, even if it is just a reminder. We are thinking to remind the omnipresent, the omnipotent, the all-remembering of something which we think He has forgotten! Babuji said, "No it is not to be viewed in that way, as impertinence." But when we prayerfully submit that something needs attention, not that we want, or we require or we pray for—something needs attention. It is permitted to pray. But if you look at the Master as our own self, then in a sense the prayer itself becomes addressed or put before the Self itself. I think morally speaking this should have a very beneficial effect, because now morality, even for the few who adhere to it, I think it is out of a fear of retribution rather than out of a love for moral principles, of moral values.

If anybody could sin in Hindu religion, they would do it. They do not because they think they should not be observed, nobody should know, forgetting that the all-knower is right within us. If this consciousness of the all-knower being myself becomes spiritually emphasised, that our consciousness accepts it as something natural, as something unavoidable, we become self-responsible. Not responsible to somebody else, but to our selves. Morality now becomes something that grows out of my inner self, my inner being, not out of love for morality, not out of fear of transgression, not out of temptation for Heaven, or out of fear of hell, but because it is part of our being. So this is my prayer to my Master that he may bless us all.

Thank you.

Master with children

Master with abhyasis at Jaipur

Master on Master

Dear Brothers and Sisters,

I would like to first of all say we are very privileged, I am very happy to have our very senior brother Shri S. K. Rajagopalan, who you see seated there in a chair. Many of you who joined the Mission recently may not know him, but he was the head of this centre for many years. And I am very sure he will be very happy and very proud to see how the centre has grown, as he was its custodian in its formative years. I am also deeply indebted to him for much that I have learnt, sitting at his feet, long ago. He has been my mentor, so my gratitude to him, and my pleasure at his presence. I hope he will also speak to us after I finish. I request him to stay on and give us the benefit of his wisdom and experience.

What I would like to talk about is the relationship between the guide and the guided—why talk of Masters and disciples. It's like a school. It is true that my Master, Ram Chandraji Maharaj, was always worried. He was more often worried than not; he was more often worried about what we thought were trivial things, rather than what we thought as important things. We often thought that he was worried about the material aspects of the Mission, construction of the ashram —the cement, the bricks, the steel. Of course, he was worried about those, too. But those who had the ability to probe a little into the inner aspects of my Master, would have undoubtedly noticed that all his worries were for us, not **because** of us, **for** us. It's a big difference, you see. To say that my Master was worried **because** of his abhyasis would be uncharitable to both the abhyasis and the Master. He was worried **for** us: what he could do for us, how he could do it, how quickly he could do it, how efficiently he could do it, how well he could do it. Because for him, time was of the utmost value, not to be wasted. We are always saying, "Babuji Maharaj was never idle for even a moment." But are we trying to emulate his attitude on time? We are always praising his love for the abhyasis. Are we trying to emulate that love for our brothers and sisters?

I had occasion to make a remark in Shahjahanpur where I was last month. Many people were talking about nostalgic memories of the great Master, how wonderful he was, how kind he was, how generous he was. To me it was a bit offensive, and also a bit nauseating for two reasons: memories are there for us to live by, but more importantly, memories are there with which we should guide ourselves. And unfortunately, today we have reduced in one sense, for those who believe that Babuji Maharaj is no more with us, for them at least it is true that the memories are the only thing that they have of him. But it is a very valuable component of our spiritual lives that we should live by those memories, act by those memories, emulate him by the memories we have of him.

It's no use just praising great men. It has been the bane of this country that we are always praising the great men, but never trying to do what they did—in any sphere. Therefore we build temples and we worship them, and we forget them and we go home and carry on merrily with our lives such as it is. That is, we are not using them as examples, for which purpose they came before us.

A Master is first and foremost—this is my view of a Master—an example for us to live by, and living means to emulate. What has he to do with our praises? I know Babuji was often seriously embarrassed when people praised him, even privately. He did not like praise. Why? Because praise is redundant. The only praise that we could offer was a silent praise by emulating him, by wanting to become like him, by eventually becoming like him. That was the highest praise. You see, there is a saying in English, I think it refers to when we make copies of things and things like that, I don't remember the exact quotation, but it is something like this, that duplication is a form of praise itself. When you duplicate something or when you copy somebody's voice or music, it is really a praise of that person, because you want to become like that person, sing like that person, draw like that person.

But here we are a society of, I hope, earnest seekers, most of whom have indulged in nothing more than praise—I won't be uncharitable enough to say it was insincere, or just superficial or conventional. I had often my doubts about it, because when you praise a person to his face, it is not very nice, it is not very cultured, not even in

India. And when we knew Babuji Maharaj did not like praise, but he wanted us to take his service and become what he wanted us to become, and if in that we were lacking, the poor man took the blame on himself and said, "I am not able to help these people." That was his worry. This worry, of course, he translated into building ashrams for us, providing facilities for us, because it was his hospitality, his culture which demanded that he should do for us whatever he could also in the material sphere: make us comfortable, give us something to eat, give us something to wear. When people have gone there without clothes he presented them clothes; people who could not bathe in cold water, he gave them hot water. So his services were restricted not only to the spiritual but extended to the material sphere, too. And that was the cause of his concern, because of his disappointment with himself. I have never seen him disappointed with an abhyasi; he was always disappointed for an abhyasi.

"I am not able to do whatever I must for this person," this was his often repeated statement. "I have been trying my best." Then I would ask him, "Why? If you as the Master, the Special Personality of this age cannot do it, who else will do it?" Then he would say, "He does not co-operate. But it is not his fault. That too is my fault that he is not able to co-operate."

"Why does he not co-operate?" My next question.

"Because he does not have love for the Master. But that too is my fault. It is my business to awaken that love in his heart for his Master."

So my Master was the perfect example of a person who took upon himself all the blame for other's failures. People often talk of other saints, of other great personalities and compassionate people and merciful people, who beg God to forgive them but nobody, I think, ever reached the levels of my Master, who took all blame upon himself. There was no question of punishment, no question of criticism, but unfortunately we lack the wisdom to understand his working, his attitude, his way of condemning himself for our faults, for our failures, for our not rising to his expectations, and living a very happy life saying, "Where can we get such a wonderful Master?" A wonderful Master he was, he is, and he shall always be. But what about the wonderful abhyasis? Which he wanted!

I gave you the example this morning when I spoke in Hindi. I think it was in 1967. We were sitting in my house in Madras. Dr. Varadachari was there and so many others were there, the pillars of the Mission in the South in those days and Babuji was remarking in a very casual fashion about how much he has been transmitting to the south. He was saying, "I have been transmitting every day for six hours exclusively to south India and for this effort that I have put I should have had at least a hundred personalities in the south but there is not even one." This was in 1967 if I remember right. The immediate reaction in some of the senior preceptors of those days was not sorrow or things like that, but anger. I could see at least in two of them that they were angry with Babuji for talking in public because they felt he was referring to them. Now, that they felt he was referring to them was proof enough that he was really referring to them. Because in English we have a saying, " Let them whom the cap fits wear it."

So even when the Master made an offhand remark like that, not condemning anybody, not pointing a finger at anybody, but just saying, "So much effort and nothing has come out of it." And perhaps thinking had we been patient, had we been receptive in the right attitude, perhaps he might have asked us, "What more do you think I should do for you?" Often my Master, when we went to him in Shahjahanpur for three days, six days, when we left he would always say, "If there is something more I can do, please let me know." He was never satisfied with his service for us. Are we satisfied with our service for him? Are we serving him at all? I don't mean removing his slippers, taking up his washings, washing clothes for him, not that service. The true service of the Master lies in fulfilling his expectations of us. One who does not do this may be a perfect servant, but not an abhyasi, not a devotee, not a lover by any means.

So, if the Master is concerned, if he has a look of worry on his face, it is not because of someone or something, but because he is worried, "What can I do for you, in spite of you?" I often use the example of mothers feeding their children when they are asleep, because when it is awake, it refuses the food, but the mother will not say, "Leave the child alone. Let it take or let it not take." She will say, "Okay, you go ahead. You sleep. Let me watch over you. There will come a time when, without your knowledge, I will have to pump this milk of mine into you." And the baby drinks. In my son's case I have given him milk after he was asleep. I would wake him up, he would sit up, gulp the glass of milk, go to sleep and next morning say, "Mummy, you never gave me milk last night."

So we are very much in the way of children receiving and not knowing that we have received, and not knowing that we have received, blaming the giver for not having given. With children it is all right because they are, after all, children.

I remember one very advanced abhyasi from the South—it is unfortunate that examples like this come more from the south than from the north—he came to Babuji Maharaj. He had been a preceptor for many years and he was disappointed with so many things. Jealousy was part of it, and Babuji said, "You look worried, you look frustrated. What is wrong?" He said, "Babuji, I do not feel I have developed enough under your care, though I am grateful for whatever you have done for me." So Babuji, you should have seen his face, it collapsed. Then he said, "I am sorry that I could not fulfil your requirements of the service that you expected from me. Will you please let me know in what way I have failed so that I shall try to make it up for you." It is not to be confused for mere humility. Babuji is often praised for being humble. This is not just a statement of a humble man seeking wisdom from you. It was a genuine cry of his heart that this man feels he has not received what he should feel, or what he should have received, therefore I am culpable. He felt culpability. And that was the cause of his face becoming grey and the whole night he didn't sleep, for three days he didn't eat. He developed pain in the stomach. I was with him. I berated him. I said, "Why do you allow such a silly fellow to upset you like this?" He said, "It is true what he said. He has come with the expectation which I have not been able to fulfil." I said, "Babuji, do you really think you have not fulfilled?" He said, "No! Because even though I have given him, if he does not feel it, if he does not appreciate it, it is as if I have not given." I said, "On the contrary, my dear Boss, you have given but he has not been able to receive, he has not been able to appreciate what you have given, not to feel it. Whose fault is it?" He said, "You are only trying to satisfy me." I said, " Yes! You are making a profound mistake in putting upon yourself the blame for another man's stupidity." But that was his attitude. He was not like us, a man of this world. He firmly believed that he had given what he had given and it was really given, only when one who received it, felt it, appreciated it, and said, "Yes! Thank you. I have received it." It is very much like the registered post mentality. That you send something by registered post, 'Acknowledgement Due' and until you get the AD card, you are on tenterhooks. He very much believed in this acknowledgement being signed, sealed, and delivered back to him. "I am grateful to you." Not even grateful. "I have received."

So, in one sense, I am using the example of my Master because that is the only example I have. Lalaji, I have not known, except from what Babuji said of him. Lalaji was similarly concerned except that he was not so open in his feelings. He was more able to control himself, not to reveal himself, more of a stoic, shall we say, more of an adept in concealing his feelings, because in his time, too, Babuji said if there was satsangh at seven o'clock often there was nobody for satsangh. But Lalaji did not give up. He sat on his *asan*, imagined that his group of abhyasis or whoever it was were in front of him, and did his transmission for forty minutes or forty-five minutes, then went out for a walk. He said, "That they are not here does not mean that I have a right to deny them what I have to give them." Nevertheless, he must also have been disappointed that they were not there physically in front of him.

Certain things need your presence. I don't wish to talk about myself, but just as an example I may say, once Babuji came to Madras and on the way from the airport to my house he whispered into my ear, "I have come only for you this time." Then when we went home he said, "You remember that thing which I was supposed to do for you. Lalaji is in a hurry. He wants me to complete it. So I have come myself."

I said, "Could you not have done it from Shahjahanpur?"

He said, "Certain things can only be done face to face." And at the higher levels it has to be face to face.

So please remember, if you are not present for satsangh, you will deny yourself the opportunity of the higher advancement that is promised under the Sahaj Marg system. Because without your presence the higher things cannot be done.

So all these disciplinary measures which we think of as irksome and troublesome and interfering with our freedom—I'm always tempted to think of the French for their ideas of freedom. But we also share it. And when we use our offices and businesses and so many other things, our families, as excuses for not being here, who is the loser? You must remember that spirituality is a not merely a sacred thing, it's a serious thing. And when Babuji said such a thing shall not happen again, *mukti* shall not be so cheap ever for the next perhaps *yugas*, he was not making a joke. It was not something to taunt us with or tempt us with. It was a serious statement of a serious purpose. Here and now you have the opportunity. The door is open. Those who don't go in now shall be denied for Heaven knows how many thousands of years.

I know in the south there is this tradition of the *Vaikunta Vaasal*, the door that leads to Vaikunta, the Heaven, in all our temples we have this door which is opened once a year on Vaikunta *Ekadasi* day, and people in the thousands are queuing up there for the door to be opened. Just to walk through a door in a temple wall! But here the door is open, which is a real door into a real Heaven promised by a real Master of a real calibre. But just because it is always open, we ignore it. There is always a temptation. It is like a sale. The whole of Europe, the whole of the Western world knows the psychology. You put up a sale, mark down the prices and people are mad and go crazy to buy it. But if you mark down cheaper for all the time of the year, nobody will buy it. So does it mean we should close the door for three hundred and sixty four days and open it only on one day? No, says the Master. No, says the spiritual law. Your door shall always be open. In fact, Babuji went to the extent of saying, "My house has no doors." Because the preceptor about whom I referred some moments back wrote a letter to Babuji and said, "I have found three other people at least who can give me the service as you can give me. So I have proposed to attach myself to one of them and therefore I do not wish to continue with you. Please forgive me. I would request you to accept my resignation, but in case I should decide to come back, I hope your doors will be open to me." Babuji wrote to him beautifully. He said, "If there is someone who can give you better service than I am able to, please go ahead. And if you achieve it, I shall be pleased to know who it is. And as far as the door being opened for you when you come back, my house has no doors."

Now, when we make things very simple, very easy, very easily accessible, people don't value it so much. But this is an educational programme. We have to teach people how to value what they have got. It is not enough to say, "Throw not pearls before a swine." We have to educate the swine to know that it is a pearl that we are throwing away. Swine have to be made into human beings. So we go one step, several steps, many steps beyond what other religions have ever done in the past. They may have had compassion. We have effective compassion. They had mercy. We have real mercy. They had charity. We have unbounded charity. They could help. We can do anything.

So it is not enough to just worry about the Master or his health and superficial, conventional, social etiquettes like that. What can I do to keep him happy? Babuji Maharaj always said, "If people would give me the freedom to work as I choose and if they would but keep me happy, let them see what I can do for them." His constraints were not constraints on his capacity. They were constraints placed on his capacity by us. When he was wanting to give us a palace, we wanted hutment. When he wanted to give us diamonds and rubies, we wanted a kilo of rice. When he wanted to give us a non-corporeal existence in utter Bliss we wanted a prolongation of this miserable human life. So who is to blame? Therefore the time is always there that we have to pull ourselves up by our bootstraps again and again, re-evaluate the reasons for coming here, re-evaluate why we are here, what for we are here, how serious we are about it, not just a brotherhood.

I often feel we made a mistake in talking about brotherhood. What for? A brotherhood which is composed of stupid people is no better than a non-brotherhood. We want a brotherhood of pious aspirants, sincere aspirants, serious aspirants, for whom the Ultimate is the goal. That is the purpose of the Master's existence. That is the thrust of his service for us. That is what he is thinking about all the time and if he is worried, he is worried because that Ultimacy is eluding us. Please remember, it is not because of him, it is because of us.

I pray that all of us may have the necessary wisdom to know what we are doing, why we are doing it, how we should do it, why we should do it, and to what purpose! Let us not forget the purpose for which we are here. I pray that we may ever remember him gratefully, and seek his mercy, compassion, and love and not worry about him. Let us worry about ourselves

Thank you.

On the Utsav

Dear Brothers and Sisters,

We have come to the conclusion of our celebrations of my Beloved Master's Birth Anniversary celebration here in Jaipur. It has been a wonderful celebration from all angles. There has been a very special spiritual atmosphere, surcharged with love, surcharged with a certain amount of emotion, which is normal on these occasions, and the organisation has been very good, the discipline of a high order, and you must have felt that the meditation sittings, especially on the 29th April morning, and the 30th April morning were something out of this world. These are essential signs that there is something very special in attending a *bhandara* like this, where the grace of the Master flows in abundance because we bring to such occasions an attitude of love, an attitude of reverence, and much more important, an attitude of remembrance of Him whom we love so much, to whom we are indebted so much, who has given us so much, who has sacrificed his love for us, his life for us and who lived solely for our existence.

That is why my Master used to say that attending such functions is of the highest importance. Of course, those who cannot afford to travel long distances are exempt, because after all, economic considerations do play a part in our life.

Talk at Jaipur on 1 May, 1990

248

But for those who are not subject to these constraints, I would suggest that attendance at these functions should be considered for yourself a compulsory feature of your sadhana. Therefore we have the daily discipline of your own sadhana, the weekly discipline of attendance at satsangh, the annual two or three times celebration of high magnitude, highly charged spiritual atmosphere, where we believe, and where I know for a fact, the spiritual opportunity afforded for our progress is something unimaginable. I therefore pray that in the coming years there will be more and more attendance at these celebrations, much greater participation with the heart, less of sight–seeing, for instance, because as Babuji Maharaj said, the glories of that which lies in the universe of the inner self exceed by far anything that you can see outside in the outside world.

People look to the outside only because they have not looked into the inside. When we look into the inside and see the vastness of the universe that is inside, the spiritual universe with its glories, nothing to deface that glory; there is no disease, no sickness, no illness, no corruption, no vice, only absolute glory, absolute beauty, absolute truth, I believe we shall never again turn to the outside universe, one who has seen this inner vision of the Almighty, which is our own self.

Therefore spiritual dharma says: God realisation is only Self realisation. One who has seen closes his eyes forever, which is what we call *mukti*, liberation in the shorter sense. It does not mean that we become blind, but our attention, our love is all now directed inwards, into our inner self. Other than that we need nothing. I pray to our Almighty and Beloved Master that he may shower his grace upon all of us and make this possible.

Thank you.

Ashirvad

If you permit me to say so, it has decreased my faith in *Ashirvad*, because time and again, I mean half the sequence is *Ashirvad, Ayushmaanbhava, Vijayibhava,* all sorts of funny things, given by saints and sinners alike. The ungiven ashirvad seems to work better than the given ashirvad. I asked Babuji Maharaj once how ashirvad works. He said, "Nobody can bless you with anything which you are not deserving of." That means if Nature, which is our own inner nature of the past, has fixed a short life for someone, God forbid, no "ayushmanbhava" business is going to work to extend his life even by one second. Then I asked Babuji, "What about *shaap*?" Because shaap always seems to work. If history and Purana have to be believed, every time some rishi went around cursing, the curse took effect immediately. He said, "Those were curses of a general nature." Because he said, "If there is a very special curse, such as somebody should be a leper or somebody should die in a fire accident," he said, "If it is not in that person's samskara, shaap also will not work." Thank Heavens! So all that it means is that blessings, if conferred by someone of elderly age or attainments, brings forth what we have in our samskaras ourselves. It advances into the present. And so-called shaap or curse, it also works in same way.

So it is futile to go to saints either for curses or blessings because they only advance for us what

---

Talk at Jaipur on 1 May, 1990

is in our destiny, what we have created in our destiny. Why I am saying this is, the responsibilities of our future commencing from now is very much our own. There are certain exceptions like our Babuji Maharaj...[break in tape] He said, "Don't add years to your life, add life to your years." A long life stupidly lived, carelessly lived, uselessly lived is of no use to anybody, including the liver himself, whereas a short life full of events, full of happiness, full of guided purpose, like Shankaracharya, Swami Vivekananda, had purposeful lives, meaningful lives, useful lives, so our *ashirvad,* if at all we seek any, should be, "Master, bless us to live a life which will be useful to you, to the Mission," not even society. We don't know what is good for society. So we leave it to the Master, let him decide the purpose of our existence, and in that purpose of our existence, let him make us successful, happy, fulfilling. I think this is the only blessing we should ever seek. Any other blessing is anti-nature, purposeless, stupid and foolish. So I would better request my brothers and sisters that in future if they ever want blessings, they should ask for only one blessing, "Oh! Master, bless me with a life of purpose which shall be your purpose. May I live in your service. May that service be to your satisfaction," that should be all.

I am speaking in this rather, not negative, but unappetising fashion, because I find in our Mission there are so many developments of which most of you are unaware. Most of you are unaware because you don't care to be aware. Many don't take care to be aware because they don't want to be involved. All the time they are preaching about one Master, one

Mission, and one Method and also talking of the method being the Master so that all are one. Only one. The man, the Mission, and all the same entity we call the Master.

I think it is like a house. If you don't look at repairs, even if you are a tenant, like we are tenants of this wonderful body of ours. Yet on one extreme, we are over careful of our health, of our appearance. The food market is full of health foods and cosmetics. That is not enough. Appearance is also necessary, they say. So these two industries have flourishing businesses and this is for a silly body of flesh and blood. If you cut open your own finger and the blood flows, most of the women here would fall unconscious; they cannot see the sight of blood which is the life blood flowing in the circulatory system. If you vomit, you cannot tolerate yourself. Sometimes it is so awful and nauseating that the vomiter himself starts to vomit again because of the vomit. At the other alimentary system, whatever is thrown out is untouchable. Yet we are treating the body as something great, the source of all pleasure, the source of our satisfaction, wasting money on it, wasting energy on it, languishing to an extreme extent for getting that. The Master, who is a tenant inside, is a real person, who should be looked after. It is like sometimes our white-washers, painters come, throw the furniture out, put it on the chair in the sun and start painting the house. They couldn't care less. We have only to pay money for all this. Suddenly somebody realises, "Baba, all this we have preserved." And then he comes and apologises, "For a few minutes more, sir! I am just finishing."

Why I say this is, some care is necessary that, above pleasure, one of the most important needs is to keep the body in sufficient repair so that it could take us across this *samsara sagar* from one shore to the other shore, the ocean of existence. The boat in any case should not leak. It doesn't have to be beautiful. It doesn't have to appear strong. It is enough if it can float you across the ocean of existence from this shore, which you call this existence, to that shore which you call brighter world. Minimum repair, minimum maintenance. This minimum repair and minimum maintenance in Mission, which is our home, also is needed. Unfortunately, by and large, except for a group of persons, few people seem to be concerned about what is going on. There is a certain arrogance which says, "If you want my help, ask for it." I can understand that people want to be asked, "Mr. So-and-so. Will you please help me in drafting this letter?" "Miss So-and-so, will you please help me in writing this?" Superficial, hypocritical requests. This is an importation from the Occidental mode of behaviour. "Please type this letter." But if the Mission is yours—My master, My mission, My method—it is your business to find out what needs to be repaired, what needs to be maintained, what needs to be kept in order; where the oil, where the grease is needed.

This is unfortunately very sadly lacking. There is no awareness in our Mission's abhyasis of anything concerning the Mission, except comfort and food when they come for the celebrations like this, which really means that they are making demands on the Mission, not giving anything of themselves, though now I am not talking of money. Please understand that money is very important, but not all important. What I need, what your Mission needs, is your heartfelt support for going through trials and tribulations of which you are not even aware, and don't want to be aware. Perhaps you feel that what you are not aware of will not concern you, will not involve you, will not affect you.

It is like the story about the ostrich who stood under his feathers, believing that it cannot be seen because it cannot see anything, or about a sailor who goes to sea but has the fear of water, and goes to sleep imagining that the boat will sail itself. He might find himself thirty fathoms below. I am quite concerned, there are certain people who have been opposing the stated will and wishes of my Master Babuji Maharaj. There is a litigation between the Mission and myself personally, as you all know. It is not enough for some of you to contribute towards the big expenses. I am grateful to those persons who have been maintaining the legal ship afloat, and I have to perhaps caution them that they need to continue for many years more. We are at the lowest level of a crucial ladder, and many ladders have to be climbed. When this litigation started, I was warned by our brother Chaturvedi, who said, "Brother, this will take thirty years and perhaps thirty lakhs before you see the end to this litigation. It is better to surrender to the opposition. What are you going to lose? Some ashrams, some land? If you are a representative of your Master, which I know you are, you can recreate the whole edifice in another name, another form. Why are you wanting to fight this stupid litigation?"

I wanted to take this advice, first of all because I was born as a Brahmin and generally don't know how to fight, because fighting is an art. You learn from the Mahabharat how to be ruthless in the war. We are not capable of that ruthlessness for two reasons. One, because I am born a Brahmin. Second, because my Master made me into a useless *kayasth*. I am a useless kayasth and a useless Brahmin both, a combination which is very unnecessary, unfortunate and useless. And I am fighting useful kayasth who are Brahmins, like Dronacharya, not killing and leaving men from behind, as we saw in the last episode of Mahabharat where Arjuna's sons were slaughtered. So here is an opposition of a few persons who are ruthless. They don't care a damn for dharma, but our people are about fifteen thousand strong. We are going about this in a very ritualistic, meticulously brahminic way. It's good that you should do so. I am not for a moment suggesting that we should ape them and go in a vociferous way of fighting. Babuji Maharaj has written, "Either return with the shield or on the shield." There is no third way.

This is the message of my Master. I wonder where he got it from. Whether from the Gita, which is ruthless, devastatingly straightforward war technique: If you have to fight, fight till the end. You see, we have to fight. There is no use in brooding on who the opposition is. I am telling you all this for the first time in nine years, not because I cannot wait for ninety years or nine hundred years, but because already nine years have passed and we are still at the beginning after ten years. Lot of time has gone by, lot of money has been spent. Still we are at the very beginning.

So it makes very depressing situations when I find only three or four people taking interest. This morning, I had something almost like a vision when I started satsangh in which I found I was taken like a dead body. Why like a dead body? A dead body, with its head cut off, with its arms cut off, with its legs cut off, and only the torso remaining, and yet that is moving, I don't know how, in a miraculous way, moving by itself. I don't know what my Master Babuji Maharaj said, in one celebration, it is in his message: "I have been working alone all these years and the result is there before you to see." Now it may sound arrogant to repeat that, but I have to say that there is very less assistance that makes not my position difficult. My position is not one for you to worry about, but it makes a hole in the Mission and the Mission is a boat in which you are sailing. I hope and I believe most of you are committed to such an extent that you cannot leave the ship. I hope that is true, that you are committed to such an extent, that you cannot leave the ship, jumping out, and saying you all are afraid of sharks. ... *[inaudible]*

As I see today, before we get up from this session, it is to try to impress upon you the seriousness of the matter that is facing our Mission, to remind you of a message that Babuji gave to brother N. S. Rao, who was living very close in those days. I think it was in July 1982 just before Babuji left to go to Delhi on his ill fated last journey of his.

257

He said, "A great danger is facing the Mission. Please pray for us." See, Babuji had to ask somebody to pray for the Mission and for the Master. And it is unfortunate and stupid of the person that he did not spread this and tell others. *[break in tape]*

On Growing Up

Somewhere I read recently a quotation. I think it is reflecting a thought by Omar Khayam, parodying it: the moving hand writes and having written leaves the blank page behind. Very tragic situation. The moving hand writes and having written leaves the blank page behind. Now superficially, it looks very silly, as if the writer is a stupid fellow. He pretends to write and leaves only a blank page. Omar Khayam says something else. The moving hand writes and having written something else, you know, it is for everybody to see. It has always been a mystery. Something of a mystery. That Nature is an open book, is said so by poets, it has been said so by saints. They cannot lie. And yet we are always puzzled, we are always confused, we are always in the dark. Nature is an open book. Babuji Maharaj has said, "In Nature there are no secrets." But Western science say they are discovering every day something new, as if it is something hidden and has to be discovered.

So what is this mystery, that everything is open yet everything is closed. Everything is visible and yet everything is invisible. Everything is written and yet there are only blank pages for us to read. Everywhere there is light and yet we are in darkness. Sister Rama Kochar just said that the truth should be revealed to all. I don't want to contradict anything, but it is like when a child is born. It sees the Sun for the first time. It sees its mother for the first time. It sees the world for the first time in its existence. It is not as if the Sun is born with the child, or the world created with the child. That is why when the youth and the old age mingle, we see the optimism and the freshness of youth mingling with the pessimism and the decrepitude of old age. One sees the world new as if created for them. The other is disenchanted with what they have seen. Desperate, disillusioned, because what they saw when they were born they are not able to see today when they are perhaps dying. The freshness, the beauty, the uniqueness of nature, the oneness of all things. And the secret, perhaps, or the cause lies in the fact that we are progressively separating ourselves from nature, from truth, from reality as we grow up. It is rather sad and quite a disgraceful thing that the very act of growing up, of maturing, should alienate us progressively from reality, truth, existence: *Sat, Chit, Ananda.*

The child is very conscious. It is very existential in that it is there, existing for all of us to see. It is in immense joy with itself; it can play with its own toes for hours. It doesn't mean anything else. You can see of your own young baby, three months old, gurgling with laughter in its cradle, playing with shadows, playing with itself, playing with its thumb, playing with its big toe. It is self subsistent, makes nothing. The mother is only a channel, a medium to keep it alive. That beauty, that ability to be enchanted with ourselves, to be joyful, to gurgle with laughter, to play with nothing at all, we lose. As we grow up, we need a ball, we need a bat, we need sticks, we need so many things. Later on we need men and women, we need territories, we need factories—all play. If anybody thinks he is very serious about even industry or money making he is totally disillusioned. The best industrialists are those who are playing with these things like pawns on a chess board.

So growing up is a very dangerous process. That is why in the Christian tradition they say, "Be ye as little children and thou shall reach Heaven." It is necessary to go and to remain childlike, not childish. Childlike, which means the ability of the heart to be ever receptive to truth, to be ever receptive to reality, to see things as they are. That is, to be innocent, which must never be lost. Unfortunately, all our education, all our culture, all our traditions make us bury these things deep into some limbo or oblivion and we grow into a progressive life of progressive suffering, progressive alienation, progressive misanthrope, perhaps, misogyny, everything.

One reason I gave that idea that the Master **is** my heart, not just somebody who resides in the heart, is precisely to bring back this idea of freshness, of innocence, of beauty, of truth, of simplicity, of charity, of compassion, all that is associated with the heart. I am also tempted to say that the heart can beat—must beat. It must beat. Without the heart beating there can be no circulation. It is not only a joke, it has some meaning, too. Because if the heart does not beat we cease to exist. So the heart must beat from inside, not from outside. So we have to use our self to discipline our own self. Discipline essentially must come from inside. The great difference between Eastern, or rather Sahaj Marg-ian, idea of discipline, which my Master has given us and the normal understanding of discipline is, that one is enforced by external authority; the other is created from inside by our Self, out of love for that Self, understanding that discipline means survival. Discipline means survival of the highest nature in beauty, in bliss, in an understanding of truth, in a perception of reality, in omnipotence of existence, in an all pervasiveness of influence.

Only one who is totally innocent, totally selfless, in this sense of the lower case self-less, can really be all pervasive, omnipotent, omnipresent. Because then you are not divorced from nature, and in nature there is no past, present, and future. These are creations of the human mind. So one who perceives nature as it is must be himself part of that nature and, being part of that nature, must be eternal. So it doesn't take very much to become divinised. Not at all! I mean, as Babuji used to say, just remove the veil, and there you are. But this veil, like all filmy veils, is very tantalising. Whether it is seven veils of Ayesha, all equally thin, seven the same as one, but as each one is removed, it creates more problems for the viewer; one more removed yet nothing more visible, nothing more shown, tantalising, provoking, initiating, everything. But truth is not something to be sought like that. Truth is to be seen from inside. Here there are no veils to be removed. We have to go behind and watch.

I very much think it is like the *pujaris* in temples who draw the curtain for the bhaktas who are standing outside, but they are themselves inside enjoying the vision of the Lord. It's only an analogy. It doesn't mean that the pujaris is seeing anything more than the stone idol which is dressing perhaps with indifference, but why I say this is, I have been having some thoughts about the use of the word 'transformation' in Sahaj Marg. I have to humbly suggest that perhaps the word should be modified. Transformation, if you look at it etymologically, only means change of form. This is easily achieved by all the other systems that we see. Give a man a shave, change his clothes, put on a garland of beads around his neck, and there is transformation in a matter of minutes. This transformation our society accepts, it venerates, it praises, it values, though it does not follow. Thank Heavens, I should say. Because today we see too many sanyasis, too many nuns, walking around the streets who are deluded souls, deluded in themselves, deluding others, because it is a valueless farce. I would not like that idea of transformation to be present in the Sahaj Marg system. Therefore I would prefer—this is a humble suggestion—I would prefer the word transmutation. Borrowing the word from the alchemical world, they may have the same form but it is changed in its essence. A block of iron changed into a block of gold, the block remains the same but the substance has changed. This is what really happens in Sahaj Marg. This is also the difficulty, that one is different from the other. Because the form has not changed.

I remember long ago in my early career with my Master, Babuji told me that the Sufis had a technique by which if there was a Master of calibre he could sit and transmit to a disciple over a three day period and at the end of the three days the disciple was exactly like the Master in form and in substance. But, said Master, the disciple could never get up because he was dead. This I wrote in the book *My Master* and this is the only part of the book, three sentences, which Babuji told me, "Don't include this." Because especially the Westerners, if they see this, they will run away. Who wants to die for liberation? Who wants to die to be transformed? Who wants to die to be transmuted? We don't want to die. Herein lies the great secret. Why don't we want to die? What is so wonderful about life? Because we want to continue our life of pleasure, our life of ego, ego fulfilment in various spheres, achievements, acquisitions, victories over others, cheap thrills of existence.

So, as long as the person does not want to die even for liberation, it means the ego is very much present. This is again a humble suggestion, for your consideration. A disciple in whom the ego ceased to be existent, or has been so rarefied, and sublimated, would say, "Babuji, do this to me now. I do not wish to live this life without liberation." Isn't it? What is life without liberation? We have heard in school, what is a life without a wife? I mean, I had an education in an Anglo Indian school, and every time one of these boys saw a girl on the streets they let out a wolf whistle, and said, "What is life without a wife?" Laughing along the fences and teasing the girls! Nothing new. Only nowadays they call it eve-teasing and put you in jail, because it goes beyond limits.

But I say, "What is life without liberation?" We are always talking of liberty. What is life without liberty? I say, "What is life without liberation?" Without liberation you cannot have liberty. If India had not been liberated from the British, we would have no liberty. Liberty is only a state which follows an act of liberation. Without liberation there can be, under no circumstances, by no stretch of imagination, liberty.

So please remember that liberation always precedes the grant of liberty; it does not succeed. What you want is freedom before liberation. Therefore is this Sahaj Marg is not very overtly successful because people want to be free even before they are liberated. They want to be free to do things as they wish. They want to be free to modify the process to suit their own needs. They want to meditate for five minutes, but Babuji says at least half an hour. Because I have other work, I have other responsibility, I have other calls on my time.

I have often been amused, in south India, when a man has to go to a toilet, he says he is answering a call of nature. Very foolish expression. The real call of nature should be the call to liberation, to become one with nature. And as long as they are in a body separate from nature and being conscious of that separation, that I am human and this is animal, and this is mineral, that is this, that is that, *panchaa bhootas*, gods, goddesses, devil, Hell, Heavens, I have isolated myself, and

265

where is the call of nature? So the call of nature is ever-present. It is all, in a sense, the call of the wild, because nature is wild. In nature there can be no consistency, because it is ever-changing. As Babuji Maharaj said, the only permanent thing in this universe is change. But we want a consistent nature outside and inside. Because in consistency we think there is security. In consistency, we can seek a foreseeable future, predictable future. If nature is changing and everything is changing, and if the change is the law of nature, then we are frightened. How can we predict something tomorrow, or day after, or a hundred years hence?

So you see, at the bottom of all our fears is this sense of security that we seek with so much ardent search. Our life insurance is one such feature. I don't know who ever invented the word 'life insurance' because nobody's life is insured! Only somebody else benefits after you are dead. So you should call it son insurance or daughter insurance or somebody. Why life insurance? We are being fooled and allowing ourselves to be fooled by misuse of language misuse of terminology, misuse of the truth.

Freedom cannot be obtained without liberation. Because liberty and freedom are the same. So liberation first, freedom afterwards. Now, liberation from what? Certainly not from this world, because the world is part of nature. Believe me, no liberated soul is going to be free of this world or any other world. In this existence it is eternal. In its existence my soul is eternal. The two eternals must be eternal together.

So to imagine that after liberation I shall be in some fabulously beautiful clean Heaven, running with rivers of wine, as one religion puts it—in the banks of the river' beckoning and calling frantically away to give you the luscious pleasure of the denied that was denied to you on earth. See, this is but, shall we say, a masochistic dream that what we could not get here we are expecting there. My Master always said, what you cannot get here does not exist. What you can get there must be got here, otherwise you are not going to get there either. Therefore here and now, what you must get, alone you will continue to get there. That cannot be material, because when you die you don't take the material world with you, though the world remains. Therefore make sure that this, in scientific terms, in substantial truth and reality of a superior existence of a transcendental existence, of non-material existence, is yours before you leave. Because otherwise, not having got it here, you have to come back here to take it. It is like a man who forgets his keys at home, goes to the office, and he has to go back home to bring his keys again. There is nothing more to rebirth than that. You forget your purse at home and go to the shop, you have to go back home to get your purse. So it is an act of forgetting and retrieving.

Rebirth is necessary for one who has not remembered the purpose of life here, and after crossing the barrier of lives into the next has remembered that he has forgotten something and has to come back here, and now it is beyond his scope to say how long it will take. You all know that sometimes you leave on a journey, go to a station or airport and find you lost your ticket. You go and frantically search—sometimes it takes a full day to find what you have misplaced. Sometimes you even forget that it is in your own pocket. This is the fate of the man who got his liberation and yet foolishly remains behind in some stupid idea of helping others, or being too attached to family or society or friends, and says, "No, no, Lord, let me remain, I have got liberation but let me make it later."

So this business of transformation. As I said, I would prefer to use the word 'transmutation', perhaps even 'transubstantiation'—changing the substance altogether. It is not without authority, because Babuji Maharaj said that every cell in the body in the human is transformed one by one, so it is really as if a superior or divine alchemist is changing me atom by atom into something new. The form remains; everything else is changed.

This is the beauty of the Sahaj Marg system and when the heart beats, it is to remind us, I am here, I am here, I am here—something like that, and we just say dub, dub, dub, put on our stethoscope and the beat is a murmur. It has become a murmur because the beat has been rejected, and if the murmur is not attended to, that will also stop and the voice will be still and silent. I mean, this is the language of cardiac surgeons but it is the truth, too. Because the love voice, the divine existence within myself, has progressively become dimmer and dimmer because of my inattention, and if I continue to be non-attentive to it, it will become a murmur and die away altogether. Then we have to pray to God.

So all these are the reasons why I said, don't think the Master is residing in the heart, because then he is a mere tenant. He can come and go as he wishes. I do not wish to give the Master that freedom where I am concerned myself, nor can I imprison him, because that would be an act of utmost disrespect. Who am I to imprison my Master? The language of bhakti uses the word 'imprison Him'. Put him in the prison of heart. I choose not to imprison him, you see. He must come willingly, if at all. He must remain willingly, if at all. But if he **is** my heart itself there is no imprisonment, there is no coming, there is no going. He is there; I am there with Him. We are inseparable because my heart cannot be separated from myself, so it becomes a beautiful adventure. In a relationship of the one loving the one. It is not self love in the narcissistic sense, it is Self love in the highest Divine sense, that this lower self, which has so far thought itself to be separate from higher Self, is seeking for it, looking for it, agonising after it fruitlessly, relentlessly, yet fruitlessly, now realises that my beloved is myself, is my Self. Therefore I gave this suggestion of the heart **being** the Master and I am glad that some people have appreciated that it could have a very deep connotation which will help us in our spiritual *yatra*. It has helped me enormously, because long ago I realised this truth, that if the Master is a comer and goer, I am very much at his mercy. And I do not wish to be even at the Master's mercy. Why mercy? Mercy is for criminals. I am not a criminal.

Once I asked Babuji, "What is all this nonsense of compassion and mercy?" He said, "I am glad you think like that." I said, "Don't you think it is only for criminals, or who feel that they are criminal in something they have done?" He said *"Tum bahadur ho."* I said, "Babuji, I want that in which there can never be a separation. I must not have to hunt for you. I must not have to run after you. You must be me." He said, "I am. You have to realise it." That's all there is left to it, you see. Then, after much thought, I came to this conclusion, first, that he is my life, but then my life goes, then that he is—progressively, one by one. Like you find in that old story about the *pancha-indriyas* which withdrew one by one and when the soul withdrew they all came back and they said, "Sorry, please forgive us, you are the boss."

So it has been a slow evolution to come to the truth, not because the truth was evasive or illusive, but because we are fools. I was a fool. I have been conditioned by reading the books of the West and the East and of our own country into thinking that there is a search for God. One of the first hints that Babuji gave me was, "Why search for God? You only search for something which is lost. God is never lost." Even then I did not understand. Because we are conditioned to certain ways of thinking and we take pride in that conditioning. And this is the bitterest pill to swallow. All this conditioning I have undergone, which I valued so much, in which I took pride, which added to my self esteem, my ego, were really stupid bonds, binding me closer and closer to the untruth, to the lie. That is why in Europe I have spoken often about the need to forget culture, to forget language, however beautiful they may be. The birds speak. If you hear these pigeons here they are making the same sounds in France and presumably understand each other equally well there, too. It is good to know languages. But if you think my language is the best, that my culture is the best, you have already descended several steps down the ladder of degradation.

In the West lies the worst. And in the worst is hidden the best. This is the great truth of spirituality. Sahaj Marg's invertendo principle we have to apply here also. When there is no fuel in the house you burn coal. The diamond is the same thing but you never burn it. It cannot provide you heat or warmth. It can only provide you with fear, lest you be robbed, lest you should lose it. That one ton of coal is better than one gram of diamond when there is nothing to burn. Nature in its simple form is at our service. Nature in its complexity is a frightening thing. Nature in its simplest form, in its absolute simplicity, is what you call God. Therefore Babuji said, "God is simple and the way of achieving him must be simple." And the way of achieving him is not a way which is separate from myself. I am the way. It is not only the Christ could say, "I am the way and the light and truth." He said it after he had evolved and had discovered that there was no way outside himself but he was the way himself. He was the man going on the way himself. He was the light that he was seeking himself and that was the light which was guiding him on the way himself, and he was the truth that he had been seeking all along. I believe this statement of Christ, "I am the way and the light and the truth," was after he reached enlightenment. He could not have said this when he was mere carpenter. This we—everyone of us—have a right to say when we reach that stage. Because, after all, it is the truth.

Every one of us must be able to stand up and say, "I am the way and the light and the truth." This I have discovered, thanks to his grace, his mercy, because one day I discovered that He is my heart, and He being my heart and my Master and my life all are one. Therefore I and Master are one, which Christ put it another word and said, "I and my Father are one." So it is enlightenment which gives us access to the truth, knowledge that the truth is well within me, ultimately that truth is myself.

So this is the divine adventure that we are all embarked upon, and I hope and pray you see that you should all reach this goal in our lifetime, than otherwise, as I said, like we forgot the key, we have to come back again for the keys here. So this is my prayer to all of you. Rest not until the goal is achieved.

Thank you.

The Master Within

I am happy this idea of the Master in the heart has found so much fertile ground in the hearts of abhyasis. I am only amazed why this idea did not appear earlier. Because there is a progression in the spiritual life, if you examine the evolutionary trend from God as something far away in Heaven, from which many religions still suffer. God is not part of us. God is the creator of the universe. He is quite far away from us, necessitating very arduous penances, arduous travels, to I don't know where, because there has never been a location to Heaven and keeping Him ever separate from us, leading to a life of desolation, leading also, I think, to a more important and more dangerous consequence: a loss of conscience.

I believe that conscience is nothing but the Divine within speaking to us as our own inner voice, and when God is on His throne in some Mount Olympus somewhere far away, there is no conscience within us; the conscience is external. I think, most of the moral degradation, the corruption that humanity has undergone over the ages is therefore a direct result of this religious conception of God as an externalised authority, and human beings should not be really blamed for this fault. It is tragic, but it is a very direct consequence that, when you put God outside yourself, there is no reference point within yourself. Major religions of this world have made this mistake and are still continuing in the same trend, that God is outside. I know adherents of many other religions, especially their votaries bestowed with the authority of the religion itself, ridicule the *Sanatana Dharma* of India for this 'funny idea', as they call it, that God can be inside. So, you must be charitable, but that is not enough. Here in the ancient idea, Sanatana dharma means the eternal dharma.

We have the idea that God is within, but we have not made much progress in morality over our other brothers of other religions. Yesterday evening, François asked me this question. He said, "Why, when here in this country you have accepted this fact, why the people are no better? Palpably no better, feasibly no better?" And the idea came to me that it is because we are afraid of the inner presence. There you have an external presence you call God, who is very far away from you, of whom you need not be afraid. Therefore you are free to do what you like. Here you have the opposite idea, the balancing idea, if I may say, of God inside, of whom we are terribly afraid, and therefore we don't even do what you should do normally.

Indian morality has, by and large, been negative. Although the *sandhyavandana* says, "*Manasaa, Vaachaa Hasthabhyam,*" starting with the mind, Indian, or I shall say, this oriental sin is more in the mind than in the body. It is a funny thing that perhaps the whole human race which has been born in this sacred *bhumi*, the *Bharat Varsha*, as we call it, India has sinned substantially, I should say substantially deeper, also, and we are suffering consequences which we understood only after our Masters Babuji Maharaj and Lalaji Maharaj told us why. It is not the sin of the body which is so important, it is the sin of the mind, because the body deeds are done and forgotten. The mind receives impressions; they are deepened, they become samskaras, they harden and then they suffer the consequences of what we consider unperformed sins, and that creates a greater regret that, if I am to be punished for just things which I thought of, how much more delectable it would be to have even committed those sins? Because, as the old adage goes, "Hanged for a sheep, hanged for a cow," what does it matter what you are hanged for?

So this is a very important idea: forget spirituality and all this goal business. When am I, as a human being, going to be in harmony with myself, at peace with myself, able to tolerate myself? When am I going to do these things? Then the answer very clearly is, "When the conscience, when the voice of the conscience, is in me, able to guide me from within and I am able to respond to that call, that voice."

So in that context I believe this idea to be worth re-examining. How this idea of evolution comes as a God on some distant Olympus to nearer Gods who appear in the way—the Gods of fire, rain, of sunshine, of the wind—more palpable in that they touch us even though we may not be able to touch them. When the wind blows you certainly feel it. When the Sun shines, you certainly feel it. When the water wets, you know it. So these Gods became more, shall we say, immediate Gods to be propitiated. Therefore came the ritualistic path of the Vedas that you call *Karma-kanda*: to keep them happy, to keep them benevolently inclined towards us, not to make them wrathful so that they will wreak their vengeance on us, that they should be our friends, guides. Then you find this idea of the very important step in our spiritual evolution that God is now going in. And instead of the many gods of the Hindu pantheon, there is now a single God. The development of *Advaita* perhaps, that God is one in many forms, and He is within. This is the famous lesson of the Gita, for instance, that I am in the heart of everything that has been created. But I think evolution means everything must evolve, that human beings cannot evolve without religions themselves evolving. Spiritual growth is impossible without spirituality itself growing. As I am very fond of saying, you cannot be in a stagnant boat and claim that you are moving somewhere. For you to move, the boat must move. And the great truth that Einstein realised, that if you are travelling upon one photon of light, you would have no space, you would have no time, because now you are with time. One who is with time cannot have a past and a present and a future. He is there eternally. Therefore this idea that religions can be static and we can go is the most stupid thing that we can subscribe to, and you see the results all around you in fixed edifices of stone and brass and gold and silver and mortar and cement, perhaps even of mud—it doesn't matter. They would show religion in a fossilised condition as it was thousands of years ago. And we are really worshipping fossils, too. The Vaishnavas especially, their famous *saligrama,* which is nothing but a fossil. It is a silly thing. It is a stupid thing, a geological specimen perhaps worthy of some place in a laboratory, but that it should find a place in a place of worship is the most ridiculous thing that can happen.

So, while in everything we are tending to go forward, in religion we are looking backwards, and we have these two pulls on two sides, one forward looking, one backward looking, and we are literally wrenched apart by religion. Therefore in India you have this problem, this severe hiatus between growth and development on one side and stagnation on the other. Growth and development on the material side, for which our conscience rebels and says, "No! No! Why do we need all this progress? Why more agriculture, why more industry?" Jawaharlal Nehru said, that we are living in an age in India where the bullock cart and the plane are going side by side. It may look nice that we have both but there must come a time when we can have only one. Otherwise it is like one foot shackled and another foot with its boot on and it is trying to walk. I cannot be proud and say, "I have shackles on one foot and the other is free to move. You see how wonderful it is! I am with the past, the present and the future."

Religion is a great tragedy. All religions are tragedies—enormous tragedies, vicious tragedies, cruel tragedies, and separative tragedies. They have divided human beings from human beings, as witnessed by religious wars of today. There used to be wars between major religions; today there are wars between religions themselves. The Shiites and

Sunnis fighting as if they were the bitterest enemies in the Middle East. We have our own problems with the Punjab, Sikhs, and the Hindus, though I don't know what is the difference between them and the Sikhs killing themselves because there are three different Akali Takhts and three different Akali Dals. So what does religion do for us or what is religion doing to us?

So we can afford to be in the past technologically, we can afford to be in the past in terms of a standard of education, it doesn't matter much A few factories less or more, a little better cloth or worse cloth, cars poorly made or better made, don't matter all that much, but if you are in the past in terms of ideas, especially of profound ideas such as spiritual growth, ideas of divinity, ideas of Gods, and you are a slave to the past of ten thousand, fifteen thousand, twenty thousand years ago, of which the Hindu mind is very proud, that my Vedas were created thousands of years ago; how many thousands? Seven thousand, says the British. Nine thousand says the Germans. Umpteen thousand says the Hindu mind. We seek in religion an authority which age gives, and not religion itself.

It is a foolish thing to understand or to think that anything old is gold. On the contrary! An old fruit is a rotten fruit. An old man is a dying man. An old civilisation is already buried and is only for archaeologists to discover. It is with the dew, it is with the fresh, it is with the newborn things that we have to concern ourselves. That is why you walk with your child on the left when you walk on the road in India, because you are disposable but your child is the future of this country, of your race. That is why you keep your wife also on the left, because you may die but your wife can bear more children. She can be a mother again. It is to the future that we have many tendencies bowing down in worship, which is good. It is to the future that we must look. It is the future that is Divine, not the past, because the past is past. That which is past cannot be divine any more. It is dead. Let the dead past bury its dead. The past is *ipso facto* dead. So what you are we to do with it? It is alright for archaeologists, for souvenir collectors, for people who have to put their money in old things which may become more valuable. But here in this field of personal evolution—spiritual evolution is not just spiritual evolution, it is a totality of evolution. Education, we have seen, does not compel a total change in one's presence. Educated people can be more crooked, generally are more crooked, because they have the talent conferred upon them by education to teach them the ways and means of twisting truth, twisting facts. Therefore you find the educated wherever there is robbery, wherever there is skulduggery, because you need intelligence to do these things. Educated men should have been profound, should have been virtuous, should have been spiritual, but they don't exist any more. It is alright to talk of a Plato or of people like *chakravarty* Ashoka, who combined education and morality, but today education means no morality, morality means no education.

So if you have to do without one of these two, you have to do without education. Similarly money, wealth. Where there is wealth there is no morality. Where there is morality, unfortunately there is no wealth, too. So you have to decide between one of these two. So when you come to the touchstone of choice, of the final essential evolutionary choice, it is always evolution or something else, and the other thing has to go. "Thou shall not worship God and Mammon," says Christianity. But the church fathers are grovelling under the wealth. I say grovelling because they become slaves to their wealth hidden under the crypts of their churches. Millions in untold wealth in gold, in bronze, in artefacts which they are secretly guarding, like the traditional Hindu cobra which is guarding such, what shall we say, dirty treasures In India, a treasure is always associated with cobras, and the older the treasure, older the cobra, the more dangerous. It has many symbolic meanings but I would like to prefer to think that the cobra, which has also the significance of being a timeless thing, and wealth can be only achieved when it is possessed by a timeless self. Timeless means spaceless automatically. Einstein said, "Where there is no space there is no time. Where there is no time there is no space; they are interdependent."

It is for that wealth we must look. And to achieve this wealth, of course you need a conscience. The conscience is the guide. It is, I should say, the counterpart of the Pole Star which has been guiding our mariners for thousands of years and still continues to do, with the compass. Only thing here, the Pole Star is inside. This is the invertendo of spirituality. Get what you look to for guidance outside yourself—in the physical world. Very appropriate. The teacher is outside, the star which guides you on the right journey is outside, the goals are outside, achievement is outside, applause is outside, recognition is outside, everything is outside. Therefore we depend on the outside; therefore we are slaves to society, slaves to custom. But here, it is all inside. The guide is inside, the goal is inside, that which guides, the Pole Star of the spiritual existence, in the shape of the Master, is inside. Applause must come from inside, in the shape of my Master telling me from inside, "Well done." Therefore, to whom should I look except to my inside for everything that I need: guidance, applause, approval, orders, instructions, everything must come from inside. Therefore it has to be a very important, vital step in the evolution of human mind, which thought of God as something inside, the 'imminent deity' as they call it, without which I believe evolution would have stopped at some level of say ten thousand years back. That it was the Hindu mind which conceived of such a majestic, such a divine possibility, is our pride. But it is not enough to be proud of the past. It is not enough to be proud of a heritage unless you are a representative of that heritage, in moulding yourself to suit that great truth—that God is in you also. One who has no God within himself has no business to speak of God within the heart and be proud of that tradition which says so. Such people are the true *Naastikas*.

So we have behind us a tremendous heritage, a most powerful image, a most fecund imagination, a most, shall I say, inspiring activating instinct to search within, and when abhyasis come to us, they do nothing but obey their impulse to seek within what they have been fruitlessly searching for outside. There are, of course, further stages beyond this idea that Master is the heart, but I don't think it is appropriate to speak about it now. I have always been subscribing to my Master's thought, I have admired it enormously, that while nothing is secret in Nature, yet profound knowledge has to be given as we develop, in suitable doses, so that the knowledge helps us, and does not hinder us.

It is often repeated that in spirituality the goal is ever receding, especially in our Sahaj Marg brand of spirituality. But is it really receding? When you look at the image of the donkey, with a carrot put just in front of its nose, suspended from its own head or neck, that stupid thing is chasing the other stupid thing dangling in front of it. The goal is ever receding but the goal is always there, too. I believe that for those who think in terms of the spiritual journey over space and time, as we have been conditioned to over thousands of years of civilised life, we are not able to get rid of this idea that a journey involves space and time. Therefore we talk of the goal receding. But for me, the goal has always been there. In fact, the goal has been there without me to appreciate it. Then comes a time when I am born and I appreciate there is a goal. A time will come again when, without me, the goal will continue to exist or, by His grace, I and my goal will exist together; we should be one.

So I think, in spirituality there is this problem that either I am the goal itself, in the sense that there is no more distinction between me and my goal, or the goal is always ahead of me in this recessive fashion. It is neither the fault of the goal nor of myself. It is the fault that we are unable to get rid of systems of thought in which we have educated ourselves. I think they are prisons of our mind, they are bondages we have imposed upon us. Our degrees are testaments to our shameful imprisonment of thought, and we hang them proudly on our walls and say, "Look how well educated I am", when all that we have done is to put ourselves in prisons of thought, created by ourselves, of which we are too proud now to open the door and rush out.

Therefore the importance lies in giving up religion, giving up outward forms of religion, giving up everything to do with religion, then giving up everything to do with education, giving up everything to do with society, bit by bit. It is not a renunciation. It is like a snake which shakes its own skin because the new skin must come. It is like the tree where the bark falls off because the fresh bark has to come. So there is a renewal in nature which we see before our eyes all the time, but we think we can be fixed. Therefore we are stuck, and nature is evolving. Therefore we are out of step with nature. Therefore today we are alienated totally from nature. We do not know what a tree is. We do not know what a bird is. Therefore we have to study books of botany and zoology and ridiculous things printed on paper Whereas if you could break this prison of enticing thought that we have created into ourselves, we find we are part of nature, and then perhaps you will have that old Vikramadityan ability to understand the bees and the ants and the birds. Today we do not understand them because we have isolated ourselves totally away from nature, alienated ourselves, created for us a pedestal upon which we stand, thinking we are the creators of nature, the conquerors of nature. All nature laughs at us.

So you see, the spiritual life is something larger, not just the evolution of the self for an individual reaching the goal. It has profound consequences for the human race. One man breaking his present means, as you have seen in films, where all the good people are tied up with the posts and pillars and the villain is brandishing his spear or whatever it is, and somebody comes from behind one pillar and unties one man. That is enough, because one free man is able to rescue the others. Without at least one free man you cannot do anything. That free man you should call the Master. What is the Master but another human being who has been tied himself to a post or a pillar, from which he could not release himself, but whom his Master, in his mercy untied, and he ran away saying, "Now you let the others loose and follow." We see the situation every day in our Hindi, Tamil, and Telugu movies. M. G. Ramachandran and Jayalalitha tied opposite each other and all the followers tied up outside. Then M. G. Ramachandran, with heroic gesture, pretending not to be active at all, untying his hand and then stooping to—all this!

So that one man you call the Master is the free person. In the cinema it is the physical freedom; here it is a total freedom. Free from every aspect of conditioning that you can imagine. He has to be. If he is not, then he has to be untied again, all over. This is the danger inherent in our accepting, adopting bondages, even in the highest tradition, and this is the wisdom of the Master, saying that ultimately the Master, too, is a fallacy which we have to get rid of, because when you are free, where is the Master? He is one among you free people.

So this is the goal to which we aspire; the goal of civilisation, the goal of humanisation, the goal of freedom, the goal of ultimate spiritual verities. It must be this, that we have to become like the Master in being as free as he is from everything that can bind a person. To this we have to aspire. Towards this goal we have to move with seriousness of purpose; not serious in the sense that we have no joy in life, but a joyful seriousness, you see, accepting spirituality as myself. We are joyful when we eat; we are joyful when we sleep. Why not we be joyful when we meditate? What is the need to put on a very profound and stiff exterior? "I am meditating!" Babuji Maharaj always said, "Beware of a saint who frowns and who cannot afford to laugh. Such people are dangerous because they are hiding something." If you are totally free you are also free to show yourself as you are, because you wouldn't care less what other people thought of you. What has public adulation or public comment to do with a Master?

Nothing, because his eyes are turned inwards. He doesn't even hear it. So why should he not be joyful? Why should he not show grief when he is really grieved?

So, naturalness, spontaneity, which are true twin features of humanity, flower only when you are free. Otherwise, you are putting on farcical faces, which the ancient Greek tradition calls personality. *'Persona'* from the masks the Greeks wore when they played parts. We are all playing parts. Therefore we have so many personalities, and then one day there are too many of them, we do not know how to balance them, and the lunatic asylums are waiting for us. Today you have only two directions to move. Either towards total freedom of the spiritual type which says, "Forget everything, drop everything. Nothing from the past is worth keeping." You see how ridiculous it is when you see the pharaohs of the ancient mummies rotting away before your eyes and yet they are preserved in museums. This is what we are doing with our gods. They are rotting away in front of our eyes.

So throw away everything. Nothing from the past. This 'nothing' must be underlined several times. Nothing from the past is valuable. Therefore samskaras have to go. But when samskaras are old and we are holding on to the past, how can it work? "No, no, only take away my samskaras but keep my past safe." But samskaras are nothing but the solidified reflection of the past. So when samskaras are removed, the past is removed totally, and in the past we may have things which we thought of as good, things which we thought of as pleasant, things which we thought of as ecstatic, sad, all sorts of funny things. Everything has to go. "No no, let my good past remain, let my bad past be taken." The difficulty in separating this—you know, from the analogy of the famous Paramahansa the 'Hansa Pakshi' which could separate milk from water in a solution. That analogy or that image is not given to tell you that there is a bird like that which can take away milk and keep the water; it is to tell you how difficult it is to separate the good from the bad, even in the present. How much more so in the past.

Therefore leave it to the Master. Get rid of the past, prepare yourself in the present for the future. This has always been the message. It continues to be so, and I pray for all of you.

Thank you.

Religion and Reality

I don't know Kannada. So I will have to speak a few words in English. I had an experience a few days ago. All have this experience all the time. I slept and then I woke up. I had gone to sleep so deeply that I didn't know the passage of time. It looked like half a minute or two minutes and it was several hours. I then understood what is this *Turiya* condition that they talk about in yoga—beyond sleep and beyond dreams. Apart from that it was also an indication that in reality there is no consciousness of time. Time doesn't exist except in the waking state and perhaps when we go into deep meditation. This is the sense in which we lose time, or in another way you gain time. You go beyond time.

So I wonder how many of you have experienced this in meditation. In sleep, of course, you all have experienced it, that we think we have slept for half an hour and you have slept for four hours. Sometimes also you get the opposite experience of sleeping for five minutes and thinking we have slept for several hours. So both these experiences—sleeping for a short time in a deep sleep and thinking it has been a long sleep, and sleeping for a long time and thinking it has been a short time—both these experiences go to prove that really, without events, and without a waking consciousness, time doesn't exist, which means we are always in the present.

Talk at Kolar on 16 May, 1990

Therefore it is to the present that we must put our attention. Not dwell in some past or dream about some future, because it is my conviction now that what is not in the present will never be. It will be futile to talk of ,"Oh, what about the children that will be born after twenty years?" They are not really born after twenty years; they are born in their present. To us it may be the future. It may look like future for us but it is very much their present. No child is born in the future. When it is born it is in its own present time. I believe this is what meditation should really emphasise. Don't depend on the past. Don't dream about the future. Neither exist, as Babuji Maharaj said so often. The past is finished. It cannot be changed; nothing can be done about it. In a sense our condition of birth, our community, language, caste—everything is from the past. We have to forget.

As I said a few days ago in Bangalore, even forms of worship, we have derived from the past. Therefore it is a fossilised thing. Many people may not have appreciated the sense behind what I said. But when you take a photograph of a human being, you are 'fixing' it in a particular way. Actually people who process photographs know that the negative has to be 'fixed' in a fixing solution, which means it is fixed for all time. You see it when it is photographed, you see it fifty years later, it is still the same. There is no change. So, we have fixed our ways of worship like that—unchanging, unyielding, not useful to us. It is like a grown up adult human being trying to wear the clothes he had when he was a baby or when he was a child of three years old. We

289

all know that, as we grow from babyhood to childhood to youth, how many sizes of clothes we are changing. They are the same cloth, the same cotton, but the cut is different, the size is different, there is always some change. Now the problem with religions is that they are fixed. What was suitable to humanity in its infancy is still being offered to us, when humanity is hopefully adult.

So this is the problem of religion, and it is also the promise of spirituality which says, as you evolve your idea of Divinity, your idea of yourself, your association with this, they must all continue to move. There have been philosophers who have said that as we evolve, our perception of Reality changes. Now this is a moot question whether reality changes or we change. Perhaps both change.

The reality of a zero, when we are in school and we come home with a report card which gives us zero marks in mathematics, is very real. But it is a different sort of reality to a zero added to a one, next to a one, which makes it ten. So the zero on your report card is a disgraceful thing. It condemns you to humiliation at home, to be humiliated by your friends, perhaps to one more year in school, or in your class. But a zero next to your salary is ten times multiplied and that is a very welcome zero, you see. So we cannot just say, "What is zero worth?" It changes in value according to where you put it, how you put it. Now this is an indication of reality's possibility. When we stick to reality at the lower levels we have to face the problems of that reality. The reality of poverty, the reality of hunger, the reality of homelessness, isolation, so many things. But if you get covered up or caught up in those realities, we are lost.

We are imprisoning ourselves within our own loneliness. It is a problem all over the world which humanity is facing, that as the population multiplies and grows enormously, people are feeling more and more lonely. It is amazing why this should be so. After all, we think when we are two or three or four together we can not be lonely. But then hundred years back, when the population was probably less than one tenth of what it is today, people lived far away from each other, on farm lands, hundreds of acres, they never felt lonely. Now this loneliness is not something to do with human companionship. Otherwise we should never be lonely. I am sure even when you came from Bangalore by bus, many of you were insulated within yourselves, wondering where you are, wondering why you are here.

So you see, it is not human company which makes for friendship, this and that, nor is it going to solve your problem of loneliness and isolation. The whole problem comes to the reality that one who has lost contact with his Self is the one who feels lonely. Alienation from the Self makes you feel lonely, separate, non-existent, useless. So the problem for loneliness, is not clubs, or sports grounds, not even marriage. It is putting yourself back in touch with the inner Self which is your true companion, your eternal companion, and which has your welfare eternally at heart.

Now in religion when you worship a God outside yourself, I think in some way we are widening this rift of isolation from Divinity because,

291

"There He is, here I am." And the farther you go away from a temple, the more you leave Him behind, the more you are isolated. People who go to Tirupathi and all these big temples, there may be a moment of satisfaction that, "Here I am and my God is there before me," but I don't think either we achieve anything or find anything or bring home anything, precisely because there is nothing to be brought back. Because when there is a God bound in a bit of material, how can you bring Him back unless you bring the whole temple with you? Therefore, I think sometimes these temple robberies, when they take away the idol of God, the seriousness of the theft is not there, because for them there is no God in that idol. If it was so they should not be able to rob at all. So on one side you have this enormous growth in temple-going—I don't say in *bhakti*, because there is no bhakti—enormous growth in temple-going, busloads of them going there, even for holiday trips, on New Year's day. Now if you have to look for your God only on the New Year's day, what about the other 364 days of the year?

So you see, we are definitely isolating ourselves from whatever we think of as God, even if it is only a stone idol in a temple. Therefore progressively we are going farther and farther away. This is why in spirituality we do not advocate idol worship, because the moment you worship something outside yourself, there is alienation, there is distance, there is separation. Now this is something very difficult to accept, because culturally it is rooted in us. We have the old tradition and we have been made to worship that which is old and we have been taught also that unless you worship there, there is no real worship—all these fantastic ideas.

The duty of spirituality is to reorient your thinking to the reality of worship itself. It is too facile and too silly to say, "I am worshipping God." It is not possible to worship God like that. Temple worship cannot be called worship. Temple worship can only be called perhaps an *upachaara* you do for something you think is divinity. And I cannot conceive of a *darshan* where people stand in a queue and where literally they are herded past the *garbhagriha.* If you have gone to the Balaji temple at Tirupati, you know, *"Pondi pondi pondi."* ["Go, go go!"] You hardly get a glance of the God. So where is this worship? What are you worshipping? Who is the worshipper? Because, if you have not worshipped, you are no longer a worshipper, if the thing you are supposed to worship you don't even see, even in terms of the material idol.

So you see, the futility of such exercises in worship has brought us to where we are a degraded society, spiritually speaking. It is an unfortunate fact that wherever material development has been there, spiritual values have gone down the drain. You can study cultures all over the world. It is almost as if material and spiritual growth are in some sense antithetical to each other. It is because instead of just worshipping an idol, you worship a factory, you worship a society which is a factory in itself. A whole nation is a factory, turning out, churning out things, consumer goods, durables.

And they are farther away and farther away from their gods, because here we have our temples in which we say the God is there, in certain societies the automobile is a god, the roads are gods, the pubs are gods and goddesses.

So, starting from that small idea that God is outside and I am worshipping Him, has come this enormous calamitous development of a materialistic society, where today nobody knows where to find God. I think spirituality, in the sense of Sahaj Marg especially, our system has been brought to this world at an opportune moment, at the right moment, because we are at the depth or the summit of materialism, precisely when there is no idea of God, no contact with God, even those who are conducting worship, they don't know what God is, who God is, where God is. It is not something of a joke when I say that today priests and priestesses of any religion are more removed from God than we are. Because they are in close contact with the worshipped object and they imagine, "This is nothing but a piece of stone or metal." They commit the ultimate sacrilege of ultimate disbelief in the only thing which you can believe. That is why Hindu Dharma, the Sanatana Dharma says, priests will be reborn as dogs because they are so close to the God, they think He is no God. They are so hypocritical that they make you worship something in which they have no faith themselves; that they take your money and coconut and your *agarbatti* and do a pretence of doing something for you and handing over *prasadam* to you. Their hypocrisy is multifold.

We are, in comparison to them, virtuous worshippers.

So this is the sad truth behind external worship. It makes you think of God in space and time, which means you are binding Him within space and time, which means you are mortalising the immortal, which means you are materialising the nonmaterial, you are giving shape to the formless, you are giving name to the nameless. This is the ultimate sacrilege, when dealing with One we think is eternal, omnipotent, omnipresent, nameless, formless, attributeless.

Spirituality takes you back inside, and says, "When you worship outside you are separate." You are separate not because God made you separate or pushed you away from Himself, but because you have made Him separate, pushed Him away from yourself. If you wish not to feel this loneliness, not to feel this isolation, which makes you today lonely, heartbroken human beings, put Him back here. [points to heart] Because you removed Him, you have to have to bring Him back here. Now obviously, you cannot put a stone idol in your heart.

So in spirituality we start with the idea that God is in the heart, present as a divine illumination, and progressively we try to deepen this association with that Divinity by meditation. This is the important sense, most important vital sense in which meditation is an absolute must. There is no question of whether it is necessary for me or not. Anybody who says, "Do you think it is necessary for me?" is thinking of God as if He is a glass of water or a cup of tea. "No, no! I do not need now. I am not thirsty." God is not meant to slake your thirst or to fill your stomach or even your pockets. He must be a permanent eternal presence within me. Otherwise it is like our electricity, which keeps coming and going, and we don't know when it comes, when it goes; when we most need it, it is not there. What is the use of such a divine connection? Therefore we must always emphasise, that spirituality is not a departure from worship, it is not atheistic, it is not going against religions. It is trying to deepen the sense in which a human being must have a contact re-established with Divinity, which he has cut and thrown outside himself. Therefore, I repeat, spirituality is not something which may be necessary to some and not to others, which may be necessary to some at some times and not other times. It is something which is eternally necessary, because such must be the nature of my connection with Him who is here. In this sense, therefore, spirituality is the ultimate presence of Divinity brought into ourselves. The real connection, established for once and forever, and then we can sort of lie back, relax in a state of utter bliss, knowing that with Him around, here inside, we don't have to really bother about anything. Peace is just to be had by closing your eyes.

When you go deep into meditation, space and time are lost. It is unfortunate that we have to open our eyes again and come back to this rather sordid reality of a worldly experience and existence. But we come back only to deepen it again and again by daily meditation, cleaning, this sort of thing, so that a day can come when hopefully we close our eyes in meditation and don't open them again. This is why when saints pass away it is called the *mahasamadhi'*. Many people don't know why it is called the mahasamadhi. Because we get transitory experiences of samadhi in almost every meditation, moments of thoughtlessness, moments of utter peace, moments of timelessness, which become prolonged to longer periods of timelessness and peace. Eventually, when a man is adept, he should be able to close his eyes and not open them again. That is the ultimate mahasamadhi to which we all aim.

Let us not think that mahasamadhi is only for saints. It is like thinking that money is only for the rich. It is the poor who need the money. It is the rich who have the money. It is a saint who has the mahasamadhi, but every one of us needs it, requires it vitally. Wisdom doesn't belong only to those with learning. We all need wisdom. And God is not only for the temples and the priests or for the churches. We all need.

Therefore the eternal Sanatana Dharma speaks of making your heart a temple of God. So this is what we are aiming for. This is the teaching of the great Masters of our lineage. This is what we try to do every day, and if you do it systematically and regularly, the result will surely follow. May this be so.

Thank you.